EDITOR-IN-CHIEF Tracy White
SPECIAL PROJECTS EDITOR Leslie Miller
SENIOR EDITOR, SPECIAL PROJECTS Vanessa Hoy
SENIOR WRITER Rachel Thomae
SENIOR EDITOR Lanna Carter
ASSOCIATE WRITER Lori Fairbanks
ASSISTANT EDITOR Britney Mellen
EDITORIAL ASSISTANTS Joannie McBride, Fred Brewer
ART DIRECTOR Brian Tippetts
SENIOR DESIGNER Erin Bayless
DESIGNER Celeste Rockwood-Jones
PHOTOGRAPHY Skylar Nielson
FOUNDING EDITOR Lisa Bearnson
CO-FOUNDER Don Lambson

CREATING
Keepsakes
SCRAPBOOK MAGAZINE

VICE PRESIDENT, GROUP PUBLISHER David O'Neil
CIRCULATION MARKETING DIRECTORS Dena Spar, Janice Martin
PROMOTIONS DIRECTOR Dana Smith

PRIMEDIA, Inc.
CHAIRMAN Dean Nelson
PRESIDENT AND CEO Kelly Conlin
VICE-CHAIRMAN Beverly C. Chell

PRIMEDIA Enthusiast Media
EVP, CONSUMER MARKETING/CIRCULATION Steve Aster
SVP, CHIEF FINANCIAL OFFICER Kevin Neary
SVP, MFG., PRODUCTION AND DISTRIBUTION Kevin Mullan
SVP, CHIEF INFORMATION OFFICER Debra C. Robinson
VP, CONSUMER MARKETING Bobbi Gutman
VP, MANUFACTURING Gregory A. Catsaros
VP, SINGLE COPY SALES Thomas L. Fogarty
VP, MANUFACTURING BUDGETS AND OPERATIONS Lilia Golia
VP, HUMAN RESOURCES Kathleen P. Malinowski
VP, BUSINESS DEVELOPMENT Albert Messina
VP, DATABASE /E-COMMERCE Suti Prakash

PRIMEDIA Outdoor Recreation and Enthusiast Group
PRESIDENT Scott Wagner
GROUP CFO Henry Donahue
VP, MARKETING AND INTERNET OPERATIONS Dave Evans

ISBN 1 929180 88 8

Our family SCRAPBOOKS

by

Lisa Bearnson

&

Becky Higgins

table of contents

How to Use This Book

In this book, you'll find a collection of album ideas you can create on your own or with the help of family members and friends. With each album, we've included:
• An album sketch (title page, layouts) you can use as an easy starting place for your own family scrapbooks.
• Tips and ideas that highlight the core idea behind each album.
• A scrapbook-page variation to show you how to take the album concept to a scrapbook-page layout.

Within each chapter in this book, you'll also find a bonus sidebar, with ideas on everything from how to create a family library of albums to how to get your friends and family members involved in your scrapbooking projects.

WHO KNOWS BETTER about the love for scrapbooking than Lisa Bearnson and Becky Higgins? They are, quite honestly, two of the most passionate scrapbookers I've ever met. Not only did Lisa's boundless enthusiasm for scrapbooking trigger Creating Keepsakes magazine, but her desire to capture meaningful traditions and family events comes through whenever you hear her talk about scrapbooking. And Lisa's smile and giving nature are almost as contagious as her love of scrapbooking.

And Becky . . . well, I remember a conversation we had several years ago. "I love scrapbooking," she said in a passionate tone. "I am a family historian, and I take that role seriously." And, true to her word, that's what Becky does—she creatively connects generations in her scrapbooks while capturing real life.

Through numerous books, classes and articles, these two women have graciously shared their passion for scrapbooking, and now they've combined forces to share their personal family scrapbooks with us. You'll be excited to see that Lisa and Becky put their albums together in six easy steps. But most importantly, you'll hear their passionate commitment to scrapbooking come through in each thoughtful album.

Enjoy looking through their albums!

Tracy White

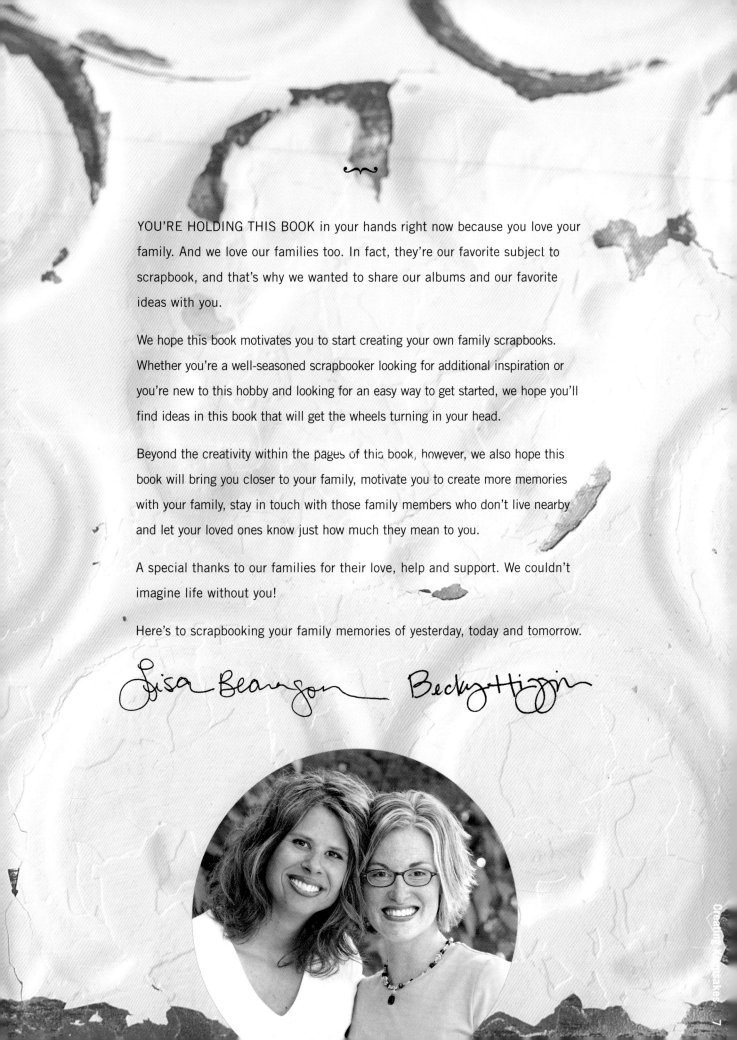

YOU'RE HOLDING THIS BOOK in your hands right now because you love your family. And we love our families too. In fact, they're our favorite subject to scrapbook, and that's why we wanted to share our albums and our favorite ideas with you.

We hope this book motivates you to start creating your own family scrapbooks. Whether you're a well-seasoned scrapbooker looking for additional inspiration or you're new to this hobby and looking for an easy way to get started, we hope you'll find ideas in this book that will get the wheels turning in your head.

Beyond the creativity within the pages of this book, however, we also hope this book will bring you closer to your family, motivate you to create more memories with your family, stay in touch with those family members who don't live nearby and let your loved ones know just how much they mean to you.

A special thanks to our families for their love, help and support. We couldn't imagine life without you!

Here's to scrapbooking your family memories of yesterday, today and tomorrow.

Lisa Bearnson   Becky Higgins

1

gather

Gather favorite family stories
into albums that can be passed down
through generations.

Scrapbook One Memory at a Time

My grandmother has a box of photographs that I treasure. But, I want my children to know the stories behind the photos of their grandparents. In this album, I've kept these stories alive, one memory at a time.

Supplies *Album:* K&Company; *Patterned paper:* BasicGrey; *Ribbon:* Making Memories; *Dimensional accent:* Pebbles Inc.; *Photo corners:* Canson; *Computer font:* AvantGarde Medium, downloaded from the Internet; *Other:* Thread.

1: PREPARE

Start with a box of old photographs.

3: DESIGN

Personalize the album with a
grandparent's favorite colors.

2: ORGANIZE

Create a two-page spread with spaces for a journaling
block and one photograph.

this was a time when...

This picture is taken just after my Dad died. My sister Gina was married & that's why she isn't in the picture. Uncle George is eighteen. I'm thirteen. Uncle Dane is ten. Uncle Craig is six and Aunt Pam is five. We are still trying to come to grips with the fact that my Dad is really gone.

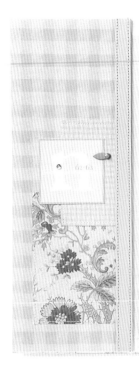

Be Inspired

Tell Me About the Time *by* Loni Stevens

Supplies *Patterned paper:* Daisy D's Paper Co.; *Definition tab:* Autumn Leaves; *Index tabs:* Avery; *Photo turns:* 7gypsies and Making Memories; *Photo corners:* Kolo; *Stencils:* Li'l Davis Designs; *Word sticker, rub-on and mini brads:* Making Memories; *Computer fonts:* AvantGarde, Microsoft Word; unknown, Autumn Leaves; *Other:* Page protector and rhinestone.

Becky's album inspired me to:

Ask my mom to handwrite her journaling on the enclosed page tags.

Write down the stories of my mother's missionary experiences before they got lost.

Other things may change us, but we start and end with family.

Anthony Brandt

higgins
aunts, uncles & cousins

Tell a Story without Words

My extended family may be separated by geography, but our family bonds still hold us together. I created this album as a visual way for my son Porter to recognize his aunts, uncles and cousins.

Supplies *Album:* K&Company; *Textured cardstock:* Bazzill Basics Paper; *Patterned paper:* KI Memories; *Ribbon:* Li'l Davis Designs and Making Memories; *Metal word:* Colorbök; *Circle punch and corner rounder:* McGill; *Computer fonts:* Swiss 921 BT (title), downloaded from the Internet; Century Gothic (journaling), Microsoft Word; *Other:* Thread.

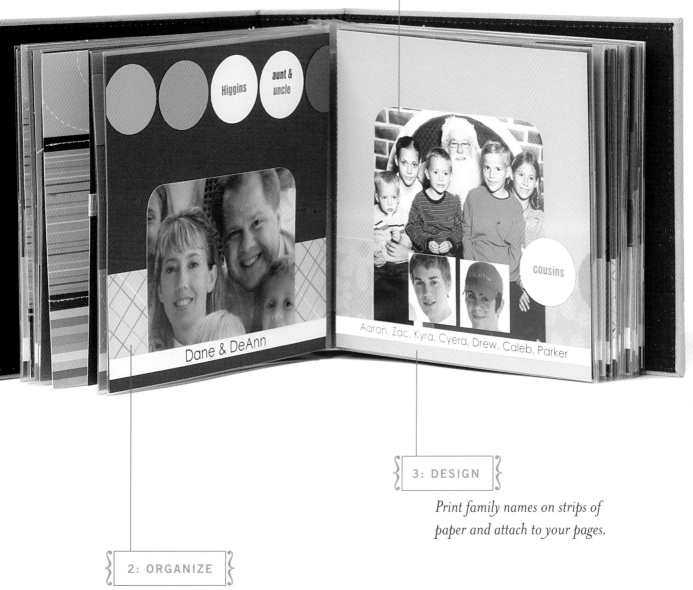

1: PREPARE

Collect photographs of your aunts, uncles and cousins.

3: DESIGN

Print family names on strips of paper and attach to your pages.

2: ORGANIZE

Create a two-page layout for each family unit.

Use a circle punch to create round accents that identify family relationships.

Dustin & Melinda

6: REMEMBER

Include blank album pages where you can add new family members in the future.

4: PHOTOGRAPH

Select black-and-white photographs to add a timeless look to your layouts.

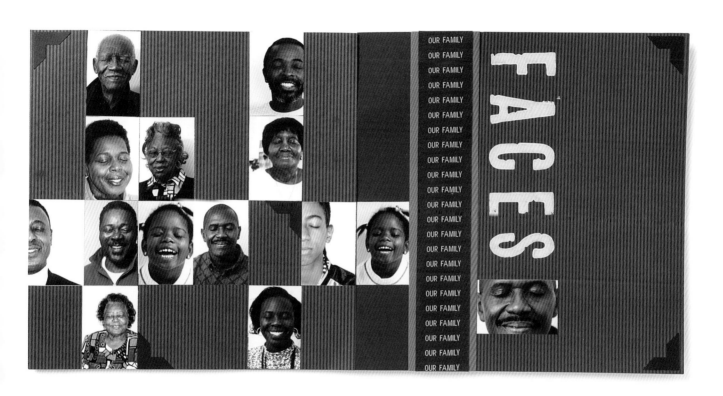

Be Inspired

Our Family Faces *by* Faye Morrow Bell

Supplies *Textured cardstock:* KI Memories and Making Memories;
Patterned paper: Source unknown; *Foam stamps:* Making Memories;
Acrylic paint: Delta Technical Coatings; *Ribbon:* Studio Designs;
Punch: EK Success; *Photo corners:* Kolo.

Becky's album inspired me to:

Take photographs of the faces of my family
members. I chose to do it with their eyes closed!

Allow the family faces on my layout to tell a
story without words.

Happy to Be Together

by Lisa Bearnson

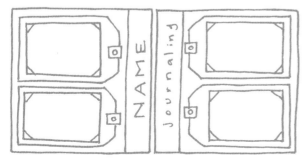

Create a Yearbook in Just Two Hours

My family yearbook is a visual summary of my

family's favorite highlights. This album is for the

year 2004. I seriously created this album in

just two hours—and you can, too.

Supplies *Album:* Target; *Patterned paper and acrylic paint:* Making Memories; *Letter stamps:* Li'l Davis Designs and Making Memories; *Rub-ons:* K&Company; *Twill:* May Arts; *Computer font:* Century Gothic, downloaded from the Internet.

Collect four photographs of each family member.

3: DESIGN

*Choose two colors, a font and one
page embellishment for each layout.*

2: ORGANIZE

*Add photographs and captions to tags that
fit into album compartments.*

Save time by featuring 4" x 6" prints on your pages.

*It's just fine to mix handwritten journaling
and computer fonts on a page.*

*Ask each family member for his or her
answers to a set of interview questions.*

Be Inspired

2004 *by* Kristy Banks

Supplies *Textured cardstock:* DieCuts with a View; *Patterned paper:* The Paper Loft; *Letter stamps:* Making Memories and Ma Vinci's Reliquary; *Stamping ink:* Ranger Industries and Tsukineko; *Computer fonts:* Typewriter, Linen Stroke, AvantGarde BK and Antique Type, downloaded from the Internet.

Lisa's album inspired me to:

● Quiz my family members about the "good, the bad and the downright ugly" moments of their experiences in 2004.

● Showcase each family member in a section of my page layout.

10 Library-Inspired Album Ideas

AS THE SCRAPBOOKER in your family, you're the author, the illustrator, and even the publisher of your family's favorite stories. Here's a list of 10 fun ideas to consider as you work on your family's scrapbook library.

Create a mix-and-match set of scrapbooks (create a set that includes albums of different sizes and colors).

Design a complete volume of scrapbooks on one subject (Family Vacations, Volumes 1, 2 and 3).

Add a comment card to the front of each scrapbook and encourage family members to "check out" your albums.

Develop a picture book that's illustrated with only two or three words per page.

Write a memoir packed with everything you know about a person.

Hire one of your children to illustrate your next scrapbook.

Work on several projects at one time (don't be afraid to scrapbook out of order!).

Have a publishing reception to introduce each newly published album.

Write a "prequel" to an album, entitled "My Life Before You ...".

Write a sequel to an album—"Five Years Together" could be a sequel to "Our Wedding Album."

Stay Caught Up with One Layout a Year

I summarize each year in my family's life with a Christmas scrapbook that features our seasonal memories, including our annual newsletter and Christmas card.

Supplies *Album:* Close To My Heart; *Patterned paper:* Chatterbox; *Photo corners:* Canson; *Brads:* Making Memories (square) and Karen Foster Design (red).

1: PREPARE

Gather your Christmas newsletters, cards and holiday photographs.

2: ORGANIZE

Follow my basic sketch for this project; it can be duplicated each year.

3: DESIGN

Use your family Christmas card as a starting point for color and design selections.

Take a family Christmas photograph to add to a layout. (Santa photos are great, too!)

5: JOURNAL

My newsletter included so much information about our year that I didn't need to add extra journaling to my layout.

6: REMEMBER

You can start this album at any point in your life, from the first Christmas you remember as a child to last year's Christmas.

Be Inspired

Christmas in the Mail *by* Karen Burniston

Supplies *Patterned paper, tiles, rub-ons and epoxy letters:* Creative Imaginations; *Clear epoxy sticker:* Making Memories; *Photo corners:* Canson; *Label maker:* Dymo.

Becky's album inspired me to:

Create a page where I could preserve Christmas photos, cards and newsletters from friends.

Keep my page design simple so I can easily repeat it on a yearly basis.

A.Net
Bought a 2004 Mustang GT
Convertable
Alix's first birthday
Teaching Gospel Doctrine
Lifting weights at the gym
Kitchen remodel
Rebuilt 1965 Mustang motor
Big bonus
Roof on deck
Summer nights around the
fire pit
Scriptures and poem
writing
Braces came off in August

good

J. good

Liking Daniel Seipert
John Mayer concert
Broadway
Guitar and Piano
Writing Poems
Dave Matthews Band (Playing the guitar
to the DVD)
Blue
Sobes
Paul Smith
Lasagna, Chimichangas and White Cake
John Mayer "Bigger Than My Body"

b a d
First Date
Piano recitals
the ward split
Wilson
The flu
Other stuff

his was a time whe

This picture is taken
ter my Dad died. My
ia was married &
y she isn't in the
de George is eighteen
teen. Uncle Dane is
Praia is six and

*Celebrate relationships,
memories and the connection
between generations in albums
that keep the focus on your
favorite family stories.*

62-63

FAMILY
CHRISTM
m e m o r i e

*Add a splash of color to
a monochromatic color scheme
to add additional visual
interest to a layout.*

2

~

share

~

*Share your family history
and bring a sense of tradition and
community to your life.*

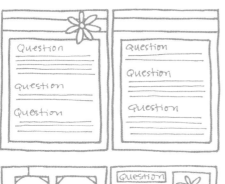

Define Who You Are

Does your family really know who you are? Do they know your likes and dislikes, your hopes and dreams, your goals and values? This album will teach your family members more about who you are through a series of "what if" questions.

Supplies *Album, patterned papers, frames, page accents, tags and borders:* O' Scrap ! Imaginations!; *Computer font:* CK Evolution, "Fresh Fonts" CD and CK Black Out, "Everyday" CD, Creating Keepsakes; *Pen:* Zig Millennium, EK Success; *Other:* Pop dots.

1 : PREPARE

Write a series of "what if" questions like the ones I've presented on my pages.

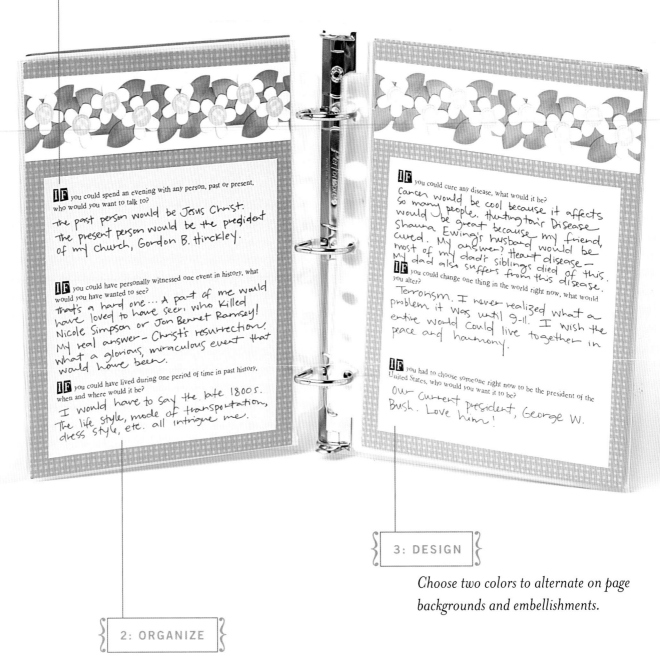

IF you could spend an evening with any person, past or present, who would you want to talk to?

The past person would be Jesus Christ. The present person would be the president of my church, Gordon B. Hinckley.

IF you could have personally witnessed one event in history, what would you have wanted to see?

that's a hard one... A part of me would have loved to have seen who killed Nicole Simpson or Jon Bennet Ramsey! My real answer - Christ's resurrection. What a glorious, miraculous event that would have been.

IF you could have lived during one period of time in past history, when and where would it be?

I would have to say the late 1800s. The life style, mode of transportation, dress style, etc. all intrigue me.

IF you could cure any disease, what would it be?

Cancer would be cool because it affects so many people. Huntington Disease would be great because my friend Shauna Ewing's husband would be cured. My answer? Heart disease - most of my dad's siblings died of this. My dad also suffers from this disease.

IF you could change one thing in the world right now, what would you alter?

Terrorism. I never realized what a problem it was until 9-11. I wish the entire world could live together in peace and harmony.

IF you had to choose someone right now to be the president of the United States, who would you want it to be?

Our current president, George W. Bush. Love him!

3 : DESIGN

Choose two colors to alternate on page backgrounds and embellishments.

2 : ORGANIZE

Print questions on a series of pages; cut pages to size and slip into sheet protectors.

4: PHOTOGRAPH

Add photographs to illustrate selected pages in your album.

5: JOURNAL

Write journaling in archival ink so your answers won't fade away over time.

6: REMEMBER

A spiral-bound album makes it easy to add extra pages in the future.

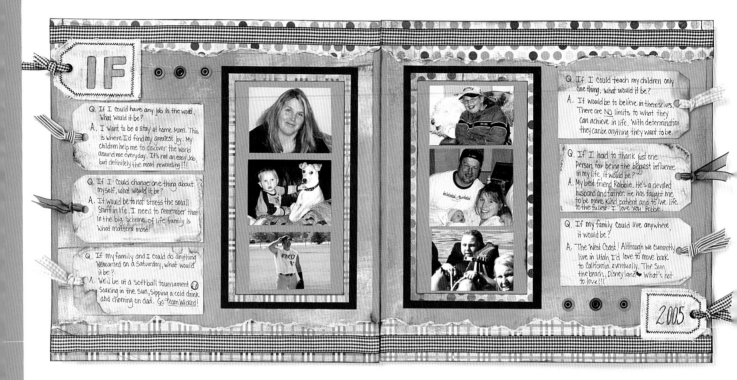

Be Inspired

If *by* Joannie McBride

Supplies *Textured cardstock:* DieCuts with a View; *Patterned paper:* BasicGrey; *Canvas tags:* Li'l Davis Designs; *Ribbon:* SEI (striped), Li'l Davis Designs (brown and gingham); *Antique tags:* 7gypsies; *Stamping ink:* ColorBox, Clearsnap; Hero Arts; *Rivets:* Chatterbox; *Pen:* Pigment Pro, American Crafts.

Lisa's album inspired me to:

Write my journaling in my own handwriting (my kids will love this!).

Record my thoughts on a scrapbook page (I don't keep a journal).

our
favorite
recipes

the higgins family

Tried and True

Create a Visual Cookbook

I store my family's favorite recipes in one album.

We can literally see what looks good for dinner

each night without thumbing through an assort-

ment of cookbooks.

Supplies *Album:* Avery; *Clear epoxy stickers:* Making Memories; *Photo corners:* Canson; *Computer fonts:* Assorted fonts from *Creating Keepsakes*.

Make a list of your family's favorite recipes.

TACO RING

1 lb. ground beef
1/3 c. taco seasoning
1/3 c. water
6 crescent rolls (Pillsbury Grands)

Cook the ground beef in a pan over medium heat. Drain grease and return meat to pan. Add taco seasoning and water. Spread the crescent rolls, in a circle on a baking stone. Place the meat around the ring and wrap the crescent rolls around the meat so that no meat is exposed. Bake at 350 degrees for 25 minutes.

HawaiianHaystacks

10 to 12 chicken tenders, cut in chunks
1 c. chicken broth
2 cans (10 ¾ oz.) cream of chicken soup
1 can (12 oz.) evaporated milk
6 c. cooked rice

Optionaltoppings

Grated cheese
Peas
Pineapple tidbits
Olives
Diced tomatoes

Chopped celery
Chopped green onion
Shredded coconut
Chinese noodles
Green pepper

Place chicken in greased crock pot. Combine remaining ingredients (except rice). Pour over chicken. Cook on HIGH heat 3-4 hours or LOW heat 6-8 hours. Serve over rice and garnish with toppings. Makes 4 to 6 servings.

{ 3: DESIGN }

Keep your page background simple to keep the focus on the recipe.

{ 2: ORGANIZE }

Collect recipe cards and photographs of completed recipes.

Add step-by-step directions (with photographs) to recipes that require extra effort.

No-Bake Cookies

2 c. sugar
¼ c. cocoa
½ c. milk
1 stick margarine
1 tsp. vanilla
½ c. peanut butter
3 c. instant oats

Mix the sugar, cocoa, milk and margarine in a pot over medium heat. Cook until it begins to boil. Remove from heat and cook for 1 minute. Add vanilla, peanut butter and oats. Drop spoonfuls on wax paper and wait for the cookies to harden. Yield: 2 dozen.

• PRETZEL HUGS •

1 bag pretzels
1 pkg. M&Ms
1 pkg. Hershey "Hugs"

Spread pretzels on baking stone or sheet. Place a Hug on each pretzel and bake at 200 degrees for about 8 minutes (just watch for the Hugs to melt). Remove from oven and promptly place a couple of M&Ms on each pretzel, pressing into the melted chocolate. Allow to cool before serving.

Experiment with photography angles to capture yummy food shots.

Scrapbooking family recipes is a wonderful way to pass on family traditions.

Be Inspired

Secret Ingredient *by* Gillian Nelson

Supplies *Textured cardstock:* Bazzill Basics Paper; *Letter stickers:* Mustard Moon; *Patterned paper:* 7gypsies; *Rub-ons, tag and pocket:* Making Memories; *Die-cut circles:* Alphadotz, Scrapworks; *Keyhole accent:* 7gypsies; *Metal frame:* Jo-Ann Crafts; *Ribbon:* Textured Trios, Michaels; *Letter stamps:* Hero Arts; *Stamping ink:* Nick Bantock, Ranger Industries; *Pens:* Le Plume, Marvy Uchida; Slick Writer, American Crafts.

Becky's album inspired me to:

Scrapbook a favorite family story about the secret ingredient in a friend's fabulous chocolate chip cookies.

Use white cardstock as a page background to give my layout a clean feel.

My husband, Steve, was once asked if his wife was a "touch of class," "medium rare" or "burnt offerings" type of cook. His answer was "medium rare." Then he looked at me, smiled, and said, "But your cookies, desserts and breads are a touch of class." Okay- so I sometimes get lazy with the "real" food- I love baking desserts! Take me to the finest buffet in town and I head right for the desserts section. This book is dedicated to the Bearnson family's favorite sweets.

desserts

Design a Specialty Cookbook

I love making baked goods for my family. This album is a place where I've recorded my family's favorite recipes as well as their comments about why they love each one!

Supplies *Computer fonts:* Century Gothic, Peach Cobbler, Cinnamon Rolls, Texas and Snickerdoodle, downloaded from the Internet; CK Fraternity, Becky Higgins' "Creative Clips & Fonts" CD, *Creating Keepsakes*; LD Underwood, "True Type Fonts" CD, Inspire Graphics; Arial Narrow, Microsoft Word.

Ask each family member to name his or her favorite recipe.

For easy page reference, add tabs to the top of each recipe.

Peach Cobbler

3-4 c. fresh or canned peaches
1 T. lemon juice
1 c. flour
1 c. sugar

½ tsp. salt
1 beaten egg
6 T. butter, melted

Place peaches on bottom of 8" square baking dish. Sprinkle with lemon juice. Mix dry ingredients; add eggs, tossing with a fork until crumbly. Sprinkle over peaches. Drizzle with butter. Bake at 375° for 40-45 minutes. Top wtih whipped topping or vanilla bean ice cream.

"I don't feel as **guilty** eating this **dessert**—it's half **fruit.**"
Lisa Bearnson

Cinnamon Rolls

2 c. scalded milk
½ c. shortening
1 c. sugar
2 t. salt
1c. mashed potatoes
2 pkg. yeast
½ c. warm water

2 eggs, slightly beaten
7 c. flour
1 c. raisins, optional
½ c. nuts
2 T. butter or margarine, softened
½ c. sugar
2 t. cinnamon

Pour scalded milk over shortening, sugar, salt and mashed potatoes in large bowl. Cool to lukewarm. Dissove yeast in warm water. Add to milk mixture with eggs and 4 c. flour. Beat until smooth and well blended. Dredge raisins and nuts with a bits of the remaining flour and add to yeast mixture. Slowly add remander of flour to make soft dough. Cover and allow to rise until double. Divide dough in half and roll each portion into rectangle ½" thick. Spread with softened butter and sprinkle with mixture of sugar and cinnamon. Roll dough jelly roll style and cut into 1" slices. Place on greased baking sheet. Cover and allow to rise until double. Bake at 350 for 20 min. Or until done. Frost with icing
Icing: Combine 1 c. powdered sugar, 4 t. milk, 1 T. butter and 1/4 t. vanilla. Beat until smooth.

"I love the smell of cinnamon rolls baking"
Collin Bearnson

Use colors that support the theme of your album (as in: sweet=pink to me!).

Add a photograph of each family member to his or her favorite recipe page.

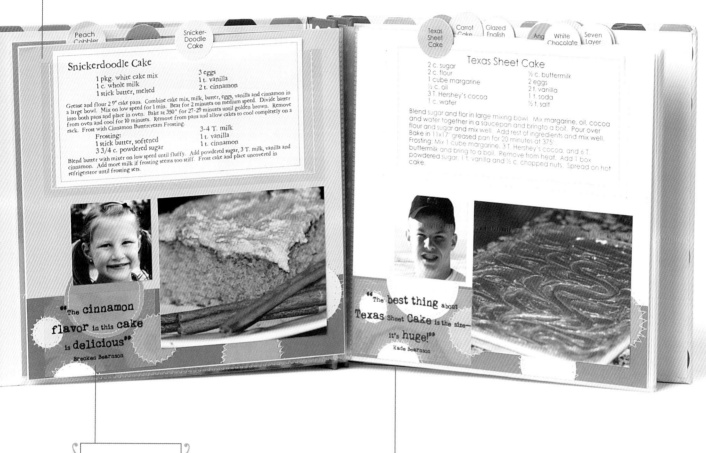

Snickerdoodle Cake

1 pkg. white cake mix
1 c. whole milk
1 stick butter, melted

3 eggs
1 t. vanilla
2 t. cinnamon

Grease and flour 2 9" cake pans. Combine cake mix, milk, butter, eggs, vanilla and cinnamon in a large bowl. Mix on low speed for 1 min. Beat for 2 minutes on medium speed. Divide batter into both pans and place in oven. Bake at 350° for 27-29 minutes until golden brown. Remove from oven and cool for 10 minutes. Remove from pans and allow cakes to cool completely on a rack. Frost with Cinnamon Buttercream Frosting.

Frosting:
1 stick butter, softened
3 3/4 c. powdered sugar

3-4 T. milk
1 t. vanilla
1 t. cinnamon

Blend butter with mixer on low speed until fluffy. Add powdered sugar, 3 T. milk, vanilla and cinnamon. Add more milk if frosting seems too stiff. Frost cake and place uncovered in refrigerator until frosting sets.

"The **cinnamon** **flavor** in this **cake** is **delicious**"
Brecken Bearnson

Texas Sheet Cake

2 c. sugar
2 c. flour
1 cube margarine
½ c. oil
3 T. Hershey's cocoa
1 c. water

½ c. buttermilk
2 eggs
2 t. vanilla
1 t. soda
½ t. salt

Blend sugar and flour in large mixing bowl. Mix margarine, oil, cocoa and water together in a saucepan and bring to a boil. Pour over flour and sugar and mix well. Add rest of ingredients and mix well. Bake in 11x17" greased pan for 20 minutes at 375°. Frosting: Mix 1 cube margarine, 3 T. Hershey's cocoa, and 6 T. buttermilk and bring to a boil. Remove from heat. Add 1 box powdered sugar, 1 t. vanilla and ½ c. chopped nuts. Spread on hot cake.

"The **best thing** about **Texas** Sheet **Cake** is the size— it's **huge!**"
Kade Bearnson

Print journaling about why each treat is a favorite onto transparencies.

Scrapbooking your family's favorites is a wonderful way to connect with future generations.

Be Inspired

Good Food *by* Kerri Bradford

Supplies *Textured cardstock and bosher:* Bazzill Basics Paper;
Patterned paper: Daisy D's Paper; *Foam stamp, mailbox letters, red ribbon, small photo anchors, brads, pocket, red frame, small letter stamps and hinges:* Making Memories; *Label Holder and wooden letters:* Li'l Davis Designs; *Metal closure:* Karen Foster Design; *Large photo anchor:* 7gypsies; *Metal frame:* Pebbles Inc.; *Small metal letters:* Provo Craft; *Date stamp:* JustRite; *Buttons:* Hill Creek Designs; *Letter stickers:* American Crafts ("O") and Colorbök ("Chili"); *Rub-on letters:* Autumn Leaves ("J") and My Mind's Eye ("taco soup"); *Letter stamps:* PSX Design ("chicken noodle soup") and Post Modern Design ("brownies"); *Distressing ink:* Ranger Industries and Tsukineko; *Black ribbon:* Wal-Mart; *Computer fonts:* LB Ali Oops, LB Kelly and LB Label Maker, "Lisa's Favorites Fonts" CD, Creating Keepsakes; *Other:* Twine, gingham ribbon, index tab and paper clips.

Lisa's album inspired me to:

Take the time to scrapbook my family's favorite recipes.

Be creative and present my family recipes in mini books on my layout.

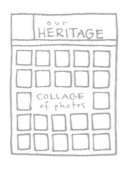

An Easy Way to Organize Heritage Photographs

When I think about "heritage albums," I often think about hours and hours of work invested into researching and documenting family members. Like many of you, I simply don't have the time to write a detailed autobiography for each member of my family line. This album is my solution.

Supplies *Album:* Dalee Book Co.; *Patterned paper:* Chatterbox; *Bookplate die cuts:* Sizzix, Provo Craft; *Photo corners:* Canson; *Computer font:* American Typewriter, downloaded from the Internet; *Other:* Ribbon and thread.

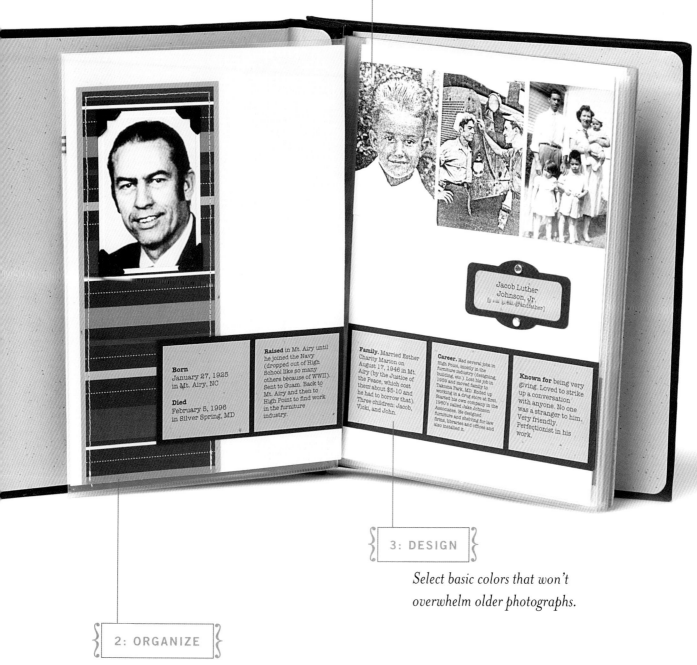

1: PREPARE

Collect photographs and information about each ancestor.

3: DESIGN

Select basic colors that won't overwhelm older photographs.

2: ORGANIZE

Create a basic sketch (or use mine!) to repeat on each two-page layout.

Born
January 27, 1925
in Mt. Airy, NC

Died
February 5, 1996
in Silver Spring, MD

Raised in Mt. Airy until he joined the Navy (dropped out of High School like so many others because of WWII). Sent to Guam. Back to Mt. Airy and then to High Point to find work in the furniture industry.

Family. Married Esther Charity Marion on August 17, 1946 in Mt. Airy (by the Justice of the Peace, which cost them about $5-10 and he had to borrow that). Three children: Jacob, Vicki, and John.

Career. Had several jobs in High Point, mostly in the furniture industry (designing, building, etc.). Lost his job in 1989 and moved family to Takoma Park, MD. Ended up working in a drug store at first. Started his own company in the 1960's called Jake Johnson Associates. He designed furniture and shelving for law firms, libraries and offices and also installed it.

Known for being very giving. Loved to strike up a conversation with anyone. No one was a stranger to him. Very friendly. Perfectionist in his work.

Jacob Luther
Johnson, Jr.
[your great-grandfather]

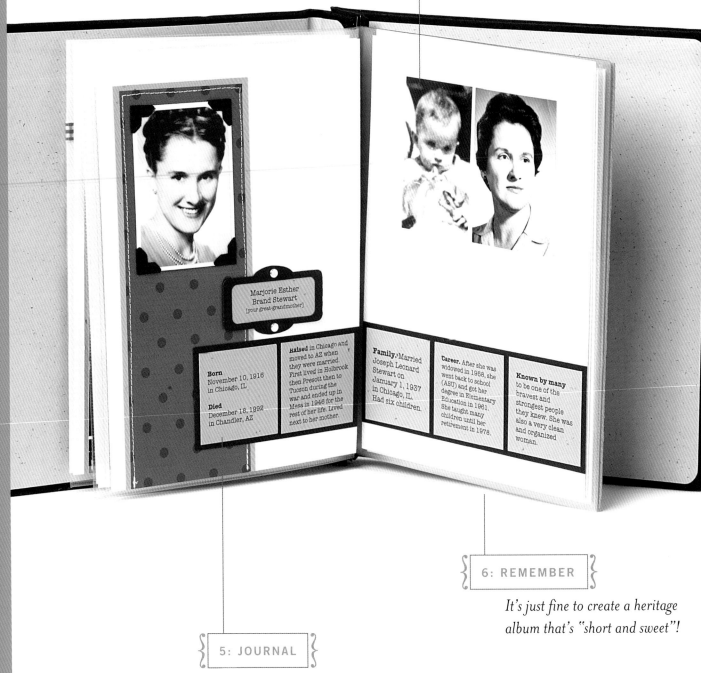

4: PHOTOGRAPH

Use your scanner to "zoom in" on faraway faces in older photographs.

Marjorie Esther
Brand Stewart
[your great-grandmother]

Born
November 10, 1916
in Chicago, IL.

Died
December 18, 1992
in Chandler, AZ

Raised in Chicago and moved to AZ when they were married. First lived in Holbrook then Presott then to Tucson during the war and ended up in Mesa in 1946 for the rest of her life. Lived next to her mother.

Family. Married Joseph Leonard Stewart on January 1, 1937 in Chicago, IL. Had six children.

Career. After she was widowed in 1958, she went back to school (ASU) and got her degree in Elementary Education in 1961. She taught many children until her retirement in 1978.

Known by many to be one of the bravest and strongest people they knew. She was also a very clean and organized woman.

6: REMEMBER

It's just fine to create a heritage album that's "short and sweet"!

5: JOURNAL

Be consistent with the journaling viewpoint you use throughout your album.

OUR FAMILY TREE

John Carlos Higgins | Myrtle Dean Foote | Joseph Leonard Stewart | Marjorie Esther Brand | Earl LeRoy Allgaier | Esther Jane Carlson | Jacob Luther Johnson Jr. | Esther Charity Marion

Harold Dan Higgins | Diana Christine Stewart | Wayne Allgaier | Victoria Elizabeth Johnson

David Stewart Higgins | Rebecca Allgaier

Porter Wayne Higgins

Be Inspired

Our Family Tree *by* Becky Higgins

Supplies *Patterned paper and circle brads:* Lasting Impressions for Paper; *Square brads:* Making Memories; *Computer fonts:* Hootie, downloaded from *www.free-typewriter-fonts.com* and Century Gothic, Microsoft.

I created this layout to show you that:

You can create a family tree page with just photographs, names and dates.

A family tree layout can be created in less than an hour.

10 Tips for Designing Your Own Album

READY TO DESIGN your own album? We've discovered that it helps to start with a plan. Just answer these questions, and you'll have a set of guidelines to help you quickly and easily tell your favorite family stories.

- How will you display your album? Do you want a small album you can carry in your purse (think of a "brag" book)? Or, do you want a classic cloth-covered case you can display on the shelf in your living room?

- What color scheme will you use in your album? Think about choosing classic colors for an album where you'll be adding more pages in the future.

- What size of photographs will you feature in your album? You'll want to leave more space for 4" x 6" photographs and less space for 3" x 5" photographs.

- Who will be reading your album? Are you creating a tribute album as a gift, or a book for your great-grandchildren to read one day?

- How much space do you want to allow for journaling on each page? You can save time by journaling on pre-made tags and/or by cutting journaling blocks to a standard size.

- Will you use handwritten or computer-generated journaling? If you're using computer journaling, what font(s) will you select?

- Which journaling "voice" will you choose? Will you write in your voice? Will you write as if you are the person in the photographs?

- Who will help you create the album? Will you ask friends and/or family members to contribute photographs and journaling to your album?

- What kinds of embellishments do you want to use on your pages? You can save time and money by choosing just one or two embellishments to feature on your layouts.

- What goal do you want to accomplish with your album? Consider writing a mission statement before you start your project, such as: this is a tribute album to celebrate my parents' 50th wedding anniversary.

a back road
in Germany

a
Back Road
in
Germany

compiled by
Wayne Allgaier

The information in this book is the
result of a forty-year interest in finding
my "roots," more intensified over the past ten years as I sought
diligently to find the origin of my Allgaier ancestors. For several
years I had promised Vicki that we would take a trip to Europe (and
Germany specifically) once I had been able to pinpoint exactly where
my great-great-grandfather John Allgaier had come from. As you will
see, it worked the other way around: had we not gone to Germany, we
probably never would have discovered his birthplace.

This is our story.

Fast Family Line Layouts

Share details about your ancestors in an album

that shows your family relationships at a glance.

Here, I have traced my direct family line back 10

generations and covered all of those generations

in a single album.

Supplies *Album:* Scrapworks; *Photo corners:* Canson; *Tab die cut:* Sizzix, Provo Craft; *Brads:* Lasting Impressions for Paper; *Clear epoxy stickers:* Making Memories; *Computer fonts:* Swiss 921 BT (titles), downloaded from the Internet; Century Schoolbook, Microsoft Word; *Other:* Thread.

Collect photographs and facts about people in your family line.

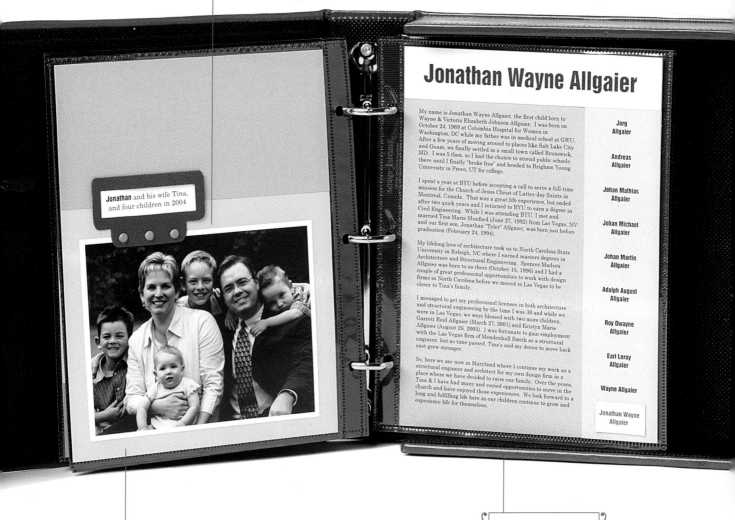

Jonathan Wayne Allgaier

My name is Jonathan Wayne Allgaier, the first child born to Wayne & Victoria Elizabeth Johnson Allgaier. I was born on October 24, 1969 at Columbia Hospital for Women in Washington, DC while my father was in medical school at GWU. After a few years of moving around to places like Salt Lake City and Guam, we finally settled in a small town called Brunswick, MD. I was 5 then, so I had the chance to attend public schools there until I finally "broke free" and headed to Brigham Young University in Provo, UT for college.

I spent a year at BYU before accepting a call to serve a full-time mission for the Church of Jesus Christ of Latter-day Saints in Montreal, Canada. That was a great life experience, but ended after two quick years and I returned to BYU to earn a degree in Civil Engineering. While I was attending BYU, I met and married Tina Marie Munford (June 27, 1992) from Las Vegas, NV and our first son, Jonathan "Tyler" Allgaier, was born just before graduation (February 24, 1994).

My lifelong love of architecture took us to North Carolina State University in Raleigh, NC where I earned masters degrees in Architecture and Structural Enginering. Spencer Madsen Allgaier was born to us there (October 15, 1996) and I had a couple of great professional opportunities to work with design firms in North Carolina before we moved to Las Vegas to be closer to Tina's family.

I managed to get my professional licenses in both architecture and structural engineering by the time I was 30 and while we were in Las Vegas, we were blessed with two more children, Garrett Reid Allgaier (March 27, 2001) and Kristyn Marie Allgaier (August 26, 2003). I was fortunate to gain employment with the Las Vegas firm of Mendenhall Smith as a structural engineer, but as time passed, Tina's and my desire to move back east grew stronger.

So, here we are now in Maryland where I continue my work as a structural engineer and architect for my own design firm in a place where we have decided to raise our family. Over the years, Tina & I have had many and varied opportunities to serve in the church and have enjoyed those experiences. We look forward to a long and fulfilling life here as our children continue to grow and experience life for themselves.

Jorg Allgaier

Andreas Allgaier

Johan Mathias Allgaier

Johan Michael Allgaier

Johan Martin Allgaier

Adolph August Allgaier

Roy Dwayne Allgaier

Earl Leroy Allgaier

Wayne Allgaier

Jonathan Wayne Allgaier

Jonathan and his wife Tina, and four children in 2004

Include a list of family names on each page. Highlight the name of the featured relative.

Choose a basic design scheme that can easily be repeated on each layout.

Missing a photograph of a family member? Use a postcard or a photograph of the area where he or she lived.

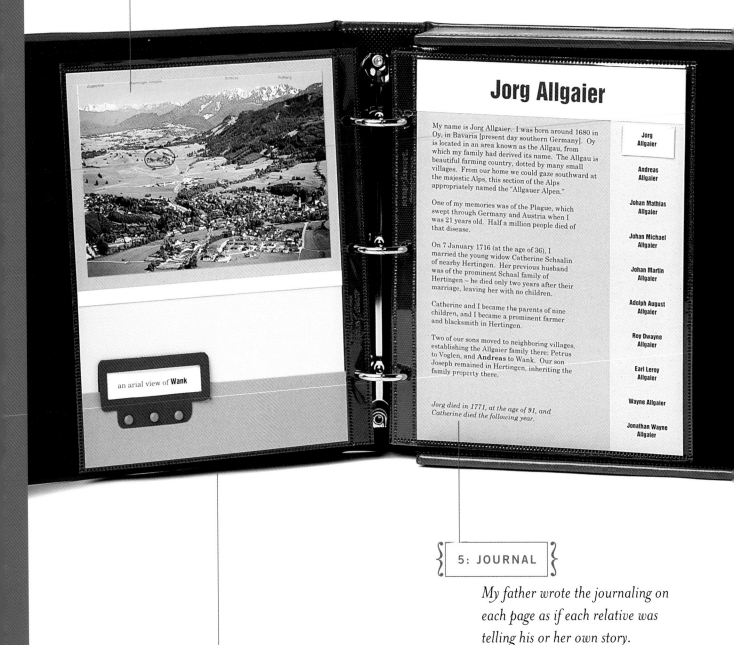

an arial view of **Wank**

Jorg Allgaier

My name is Jorg Allgaier. I was born around 1680 in Oy, in Bavaria [present day southern Germany]. Oy is located in an area known as the Allgau, from which my family had derived its name. The Allgau is beautiful farming country, dotted by many small villages. From our home we could gaze southward at the majestic Alps, this section of the Alps appropriately named the "Allgauer Alpen."

One of my memories was of the Plague, which swept through Germany and Austria when I was 21 years old. Half a million people died of that disease.

On 7 January 1716 (at the age of 36), I married the young widow Catherine Schaalin of nearby Hertingen. Her previous husband was of the prominent Schaal family of Hertingen — he died only two years after their marriage, leaving her with no children.

Catherine and I became the parents of nine children, and I became a prominent farmer and blacksmith in Hertingen.

Two of our sons moved to neighboring villages, establishing the Allgaier family there: Petrus to Voglen, and **Andreas** to Wank. Our son Joseph remained in Hertingen, inheriting the family property there.

Jorg died in 1771, at the age of 91, and Catherine died the following year.

Jorg Allgaier

Andreas Allgaier

Johan Mathias Allgaier

Johan Michael Allgaier

Johan Martin Allgaier

Adolph August Allgaier

Roy Dwayne Allgaier

Earl Leroy Allgaier

Wayne Allgaier

Jonathan Wayne Allgaier

My father wrote the journaling on each page as if each relative was telling his or her own story.

Other members of your family may appreciate receiving color copies of a family line album.

Be Inspired

She Gets That from Me *by* Kerri Bradford

Supplies *Patterned paper:* My Mind's Eye; *Transparency:* Creative Imaginations; *Rub-on letters, binding tape, mini brad and acrylic paint:* Making Memories; *Ribbon and metal rings:* Li'l Davis Designs; *Metal rivets:* Chatterbox; *Photo anchor:* 7gypsies; *Photo corners:* Canson; *Letter stamps:* Ma Vinci's Reliquary ("gets" and "me"), PSX Design ("she"), Making Memories (small alphabet and foam design stamp); *Date stamp:* JustRite; *Distressing ink:* Ranger Industries; *Computer fonts:* LB Kelly and LB Loni Leah, Lisa's Favorite Fonts CD, Vol. 2, Creating Keepsakes; *Other:* Dymo label maker, silk flower, button and snap tape.

Becky's album inspired me to:

Create a layout about my daughter's maternal line.

Discover common interests (love of music and the outdoors) that have been passed down through our maternal line.

sweet
memories

a back road
in German

Display beautiful photographs against a plain or contrasting background. You'll find that a basic background will often show images to their best advantage.

Arrange a few of your favorite albums on a shelf or coffee table so that your family can easily spend a rainy afternoon browsing through family photographs.

BE

3

~

learn

~

*Teach future generations
who you are as you scrapbook
the lessons of your life.*

Turning Points. Situations in my life, both good and bad, that have taught me invaluable lessons. Lessons that have changed my life forever.

One Photo, One Paragraph, One Album

This album showcases the "turning points" in my life, those moments that helped define my values and shape who I am. This album tells a story with just one photo and one journaling block per layout.

Supplies *Album:* Boundless Memories; *Patterned paper and letters:* Butcher Block, Déjà Views, The C-Thru Ruler Co.; *Binding tape:* Making Memories; *Stamping ink:* Ranger Industries; *Computer font:* CK True Type, "The Heritage, Vintage & Retro Collection" CD, *Creating Keepsakes.*

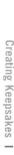

1: PREPARE

Make a list of turning points in your life.

It may look like just an old doll head—one that was popular in the seventies. Yet for me, it's a reminder of a turning point in my life that taught me the importance of being grateful. The Christmas I was 10, I spent hours looking through the Sears catalogue, marking and remarking all the presents I wanted Santa to bring. Top of my list was a doll head where I could experiment on hair. There were two in the catalogue—a very ugly one and a beautiful one. I kept telling my mom, "This one is ugly—I want this pretty one." I couldn't wait until Christmas morning—I knew I was getting the beautiful doll head. Imagine my shock and horror when I opened my gift and discovered the ugly doll head. I threw a fit and ran to my room sobbing. I spent a good share of the day in my room—embarrassed at how I was acting but still upset that my mom had gotten the present so mixed up. I finally joined the family only to find my mother with red, swollen eyes. She'd cried as much as I had. Suddenly I knew I'd been an ungrateful snot and I vowed then and there I'd always be grateful for everything I was given.

3: DESIGN

Create a thoughtful and reflective mood on your page with quiet and subdued papers.

2: ORGANIZE

Collect photographs that symbolize each turning point.

Use a zoom lens to capture macro shots of "turning point" symbols.

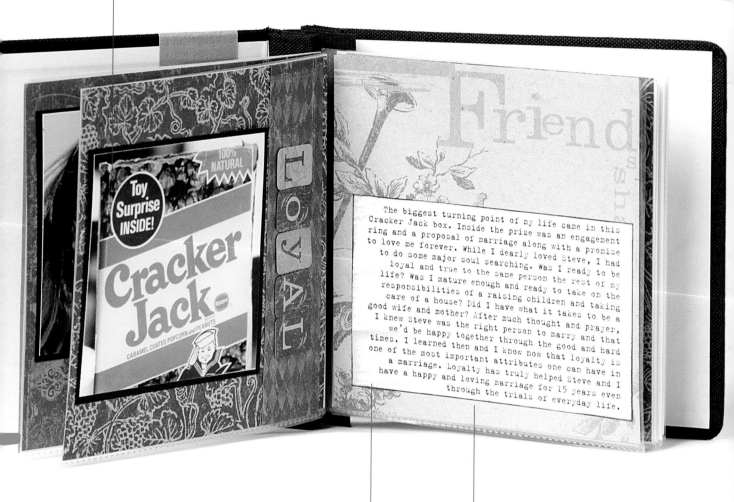

LOYAL

The biggest turning point of my life came in this Cracker Jack box. Inside the prize was an engagement ring and a proposal of marriage along with a promise to love me forever. While I dearly loved Steve, I had to do some major soul searching. Was I ready to be loyal and true to the same person the rest of my life? Was I mature enough and ready to take on the responsibilities of a raising children and taking care of a house? Did I have what it takes to be a good wife and mother? After much thought and prayer, I knew Steve was the right person to marry and that we'd be happy together through the good and hard times. I learned then and I know now that loyalty is one of the most important attributes one can have in a marriage. Loyalty has truly helped Steve and I have a happy and loving marriage for 15 years even through the trials of everyday life.

5: JOURNAL

Be honest in your journaling and examine the thought process that helped you make a choice.

6: REMEMBER

Write from your heart. Allow your family to discover you in your words.

Be Inspired

Stretch *by* Alison Marquis

Supplies *Textured cardstock, patterned paper, ribbon and brads:* DieCuts with a View; *Monogram:* My Mind's Eye; *Rub-ons:* Scrapworks; *Bookplate:* Jo-Ann Crafts; *Metal letter and safety pin:* Making Memories; *Mirror:* Provo Craft; *Stamping ink:* Memories, Stewart Superior Corporation; *Embossing powder:* Close To My Heart; *Other:* Velcro, sandpaper and staples.

Lisa's album inspired me to:

● Create a "turning point" album about my son's fifth birthday.

● Explore my emotions about my son growing up and becoming more independent.

Short and Sweet: A Gratitude Journal

My gratitude journal is an album with photographs

and journaling—a place where I give thanks for all

that I've been given, a place where I celebrate the

things I've learned.

Supplies *Album:* K&Company; *Textured cardstock:* Bazzill Basics Paper; *Patterned paper and brads:* Lasting Impressions for Paper; *Ribbon:* Making Memories and Li'l Davis Designs; *Paper flowers:* Making Memories; *Corner rounder:* Marvy Uchida; *Photo corners:* Canson; *Letter stickers:* Li'l Davis Designs; *Computer fonts:* Century Schoolbook BT and Futura Light BT, downloaded from the Internet.

Start with a small album and give yourself permission to keep your entries short and sweet.

i am

grateful

for

my friends!

Friends. Sure — almost anyone can say they have friends & they're grateful for them. It's a natural thing—that happens. You meet people. You click with one or two or ten... and you have friends! But I was just thinking — what would my life be like without these fabulous people?

What if I didn't have the daily chats on the phone and the frequent get-togethers and the late-night chats while we scrapbook? They are a big part of who I am and I wouldn't want to ever have that part in my life missing.

today's date:

December 20, 2004

Create several pages at one time, leaving blank spaces to add photos and journaling in the future.

Make an appointment with yourself to journal once a week.

Share the imperfect moments of your lives with family members.

i am
grateful
for

my health

It's usually an illness or something that reminds me how valuable good health is. I was just hit with the stomach flu over the weekend and felt miserable. It's so easy to take it for granted when we feel totally well and energetic. I've had my share of health issues and scares and trials. They are memories that are burned in my memory. The one I don't remember was my battle with bacterial meningitis as an infant. How miraculous it is to live in a time where modern medicine & technology can preserve us so we can fulfill our mission on Earth.

January 9, 2005

Illustrate your journal with photographs from any point in your life.

Date each entry—your family members will enjoy seeing how your life has changed over time.

family **gratitude**

summer **1981**

summer **1993**

I was thrilled beyond belief when my sister told me that she is pregnant and due just 8 days after me! I have always dreamed of giving my children what I had when I was growing up. I am so grateful for growing up with my cousins. It was a true blessing to have 20 cousins (including 2 girls my age) most of whom grew up in the same area that I did. Thoughts of Sundays at Grandma's house and summers at the beach will always bring a smile to my face. Spending time with my extended family was a regular occurrence then and now and not just on holidays or family reunions, but all the time and often for no reason at all.

Be Inspired

Family Gratitude *by* Erin Roe

Supplies *Textured cardstock:* Bazzill Basics Paper; *Patterned paper:* Flair Designs; *Acrylic accent:* KI Memories; *Computer fonts:* Times New Roman, Microsoft Word; AL Cadence, "Script" CD, Autumn Leaves.

Becky's album inspired me to:

Share my feelings about my close family ties on a scrapbook page.

Express my gratitude for my family.

The Best things I have Learned from My MOTHER

The Best Things I Have Learned from My Mother

by Heather Combs

When I designed this gift album, I knew I wanted it to be a place where I could show my mother just how much I appreciated the lessons she's taught me over the years. I envisioned the album as a beautiful book she could display on a shelf or coffee table.

To create this project, I altered a book (you could easily start this project with a box shaped like a book as well), decorating the inside and outside. The inside of the album is an accordion-folded strip, with each section decorated with words, symbols and embellishments that show what I've learned from my mother.

The final touch on this project? I wrote a letter to my mom and decoupaged it to the inside back cover of the project. My letter reads, in part:

Dear Mom,

These are the things I consider to be the best of your legacy to me. Things like how keeping a lovely home doesn't just mean how the home looks, but more importantly, how it feels ... I know I have inherited my love of music, books and fine arts from you, and without your courageous example to keep learning, I never would have taken up the harp (not to mention finally learning how to make real whipped cream!).

I love you, Heather

Live, Learn, Pass It On

by Lisa Bearnson and Family

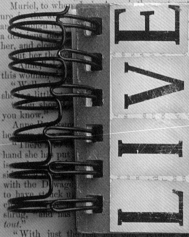

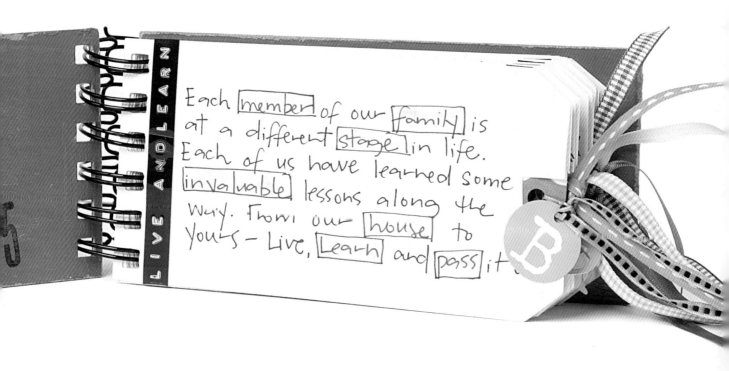

Each member of our family is at a different stage in life. Each of us have learned some invaluable lessons along the way. From our house to yours - Live, Learn and pass it on.

Live Learn PASS IT ON

I've learned ...

NAME

Share Life's Lessons

My whole life has been a learning experience.

This album is a snapshot in time, a way to

preserve what each of my family members

has "lived, learned" and wants to "pass on"

to others.

Supplies *Album:* 7gypsies; *Patterned paper, ribbon, charms and acrylic paint:* Making Memories; *Letter stamps:* Postmodern Design and Making Memories; *Letter stickers:* Scenic Route Paper Co.; *Label maker:* Dymo; *Chalk:* Craf-T Products.

{ 1 : PREPARE }

Start with a tag booklet and decorate
the pages as desired.

{ 2 : ORGANIZE }

Collect initial charms and ribbons to
finish each layout.

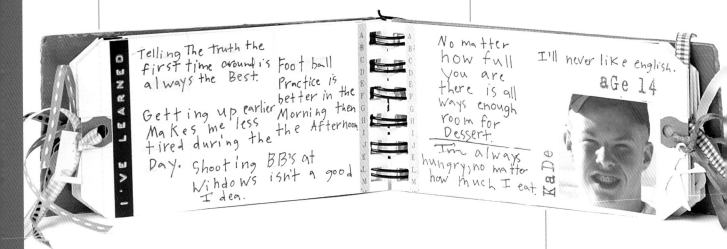

{ 3 : DESIGN }

Stamp family members'
names and ages around
their photographs.

Use photographs of each family member—or substitute a photograph of a symbol that illustrates the lesson learned.

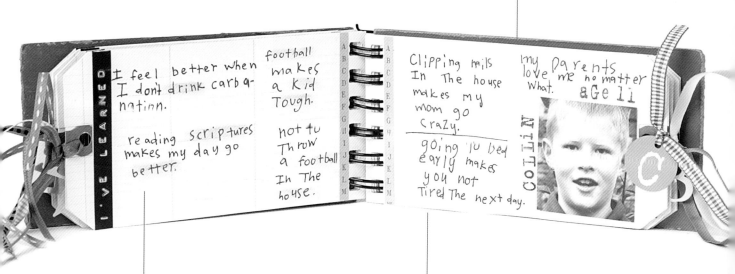

I'VE LEARNED

I feel better when I don't drink carbqnation.

reading scriptures makes my day go better.

football makes a kid Tough.

not tu Throw a football In The house.

Clipping nils In The house makes my mom go crazy.

going to bed early makes you not Tired The next day.

my parents love me no matter what.

aGe 11

COLLIN

5: JOURNAL

Add extra charm to your pages by asking family members to journal in their own handwriting.

6: REMEMBER

Don't worry about your children making spelling mistakes on a layout—it will making the layout more endearing!

Be Inspired

Live, Learn, and Pass It On

by Marci Leishman

Supplies *Patterned paper:* Daisy D's Paper Co.; *Chipboard letters and rub-on words:* Li'l Davis Designs; *Letter stickers:* BasicGrey; *Foam stamps and metal letters:* Making Memories; *Epoxy words:* K&Company; *Printed twill:* My Mind's Eye; *Word stickers:* Making Memories and Chatterbox; *Metal word charms:* Pebbles Inc.; *Metal words:* Daisy Hill and Lasting Impressions for Paper; *Epoxy stickers:* Creative Imaginations; *Metal tag:* Colorbök; *Label maker:* Dymo; *Brads:* Karen Foster Design; *Stamping ink:* StazOn, Tsukineko; Nick Bantock, Ranger Industries; *Acrylic paint:* Delta Technical Coatings; *Computer font:* CK Constitution, "Fresh Fonts" CD, *Creating Keepsakes; Other:* Letter beads, ribbon and twill.

Lisa's album inspired me to:

Interview my family members about what they've learned in life.

Create a layout that shares our family values.

Bearnson Family
Traditions

{ ALBUM 13 }

by Lisa Bearnson

Bearnson Family.
traditions

Tell About Traditions

What sort of unique traditions help define your family? I created this album as a place where I could write about the non-seasonal traditions that bond my family together throughout the year.

Supplies *Album and patterned paper:* Making Memories; *Computer fonts:* Century Gothic, downloaded from the Internet; CK Postage Due, "The Heritage, Vintage & Retro Collection" CD, *Creating Keepsakes.*

1: PREPARE

Make a list of the non-seasonal traditions that bond your family together.

A birthday isn't a birthday without breakfast in bed—at least not at the Bearnson house. Making the honoree breakfast and serving it in bed is a family affair. Take Sage's fourth birthday. I made the French toast and set up the tray, Kade cut the apples, Brecken created the card, while Collin lit the candles. Dad then joined us all in a hearty "Happy Birthday To You" song for Sage.

Another favorite birthday tradition is the rule "no chores on your special day." The kids take full advantage of this and I love it. I make beds, clean bathrooms and pick up clothes with a cheerful heart—this only happens once a year and I want to make it a great day for each member of my family and that they know how much I love them.

BIRTHDAY BREAKFAST in bed

3: DESIGN

Have fun and play with different color schemes within the same basic design.

2: ORGANIZE

Jot down notes on how each tradition started and how it has changed over the years.

Choose a method of photographing your family traditions each year (i.e., always zoom in on your child's new shoes).

Tell the "story behind the story" (like I did with my son's pleas to wear his shoes before school started!).

first day of school! **SHOE SNAPSHOTS**

Getting new shoes for the first day of school is a tradition. Taking photos of these shoes is also a tradition. Sometimes the new shoes don't look like new shoes. Just take a look at Collin's in the photo. We bought them a couple of weeks before school and he convinced me to wear them only once. Then once turned into twice and twice turned into three times. By the time school started, they didn't look new anymore. But I discovered I love them even more not new. They represent a little boy who loves life, plays hard and is always in too big of a hurry to tie his shoes.

Your family traditions help tell the story of what you value and who you are—scrapbook them!

Be Inspired

Grandma's Ornaments *by* Angela Ash

Supplies *Foam stamps, acrylic paint and rub-ons:* Making Memories; *Mini book:* Autumn Leaves; *Rubber stamp:* EK Success; *Label maker:* Dymo; *Button:* K&Company; *Computer fonts:* CK Woodbine and CK Woodbine Swashes, "Fresh Fonts" CD Vol. 2, *Creating Keepsakes;* *Other:* Fibers, ribbon, twill and staples.

Lisa's album inspired me to:

Pass on the story of a favorite Christmas tradition.

Capture the sweet and giving personality of our Grandma Downs.

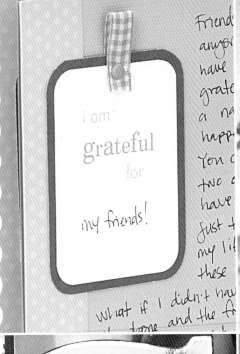

i am
grateful
for
my friends!

Friend...
anyor...
have
grate...
a na...
happ...
You ...
two ...
have
Just t...
my lif...
these...

what if I didn't hav...
...drone and the fri...

*Pay attention to the details
you choose to add to each
page layout. Your embellishments
will help tell the story you want
to share on each page.*

iggest turning point of my life came in th...
Jack box. Inside the prize was an engagem...
a proposal of marriage along with a prom...
me forever. While I dearly loved Steve, I ...
some major soul searching. Was I ready to ...
al and true to the same person the rest of ...
Was I mature enough and ready to take on ...
nsibilities of a raising children and tak...
of a house? Did I have what it takes to b...
e and mother? After much thought and pray...
Steve was the right person to marry and t...
l be happy together through the good and h...
I learned then and I know now that loyalty ...
he most important attributes one can have ...
rriage. Loyalty has truly helped Steve ar...
a happy and loving marriage for 15 years e...
through the trials of everyday li...

LADY BRANKSMER...

...n so used to her myself in ... ye...
...have forgotten to analyze m... ...gs with...
Yet it seems natural enoug... ...e, tha...
...her might fail to see her ...

*Create continuity in your
albums by repeating just one
element, such as black-and-white
photographs and/or a typewriter
inspired computer font.*

4

⌁

connect

⌁

Connect with other generations
as you teach them more
about who you are.

When I Was Your Age

by Becky Higgins

when i was **your** age

when i was your age
(because - believe it or not - i really was your age once!)

a summary of my childhood, so that my children may understand a little about my past and how it's not so different from their own.

compiled by becky higgins in 2005

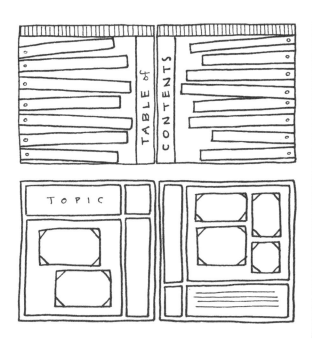

Summarize Childhood Memories

I wanted to share my childhood memories with my son so that he would have a real sense that I was once a kid, too. In this album, I summarized my memories with a few snapshots and sentences.

Supplies *Album:* Colorbök; *Patterned papers:* Colors By Design (blocks) and Lasting Impressions for Paper (dots); *Brads:* Lasting Impressions for Paper (pink and green) and Karen Foster Design (red); *Circle punch:* EK Success; *Computer font:* Futura, downloaded from the Internet.

Start with a list of general topics (family, home, hobbies, pets) and find photos to illustrate each topic.

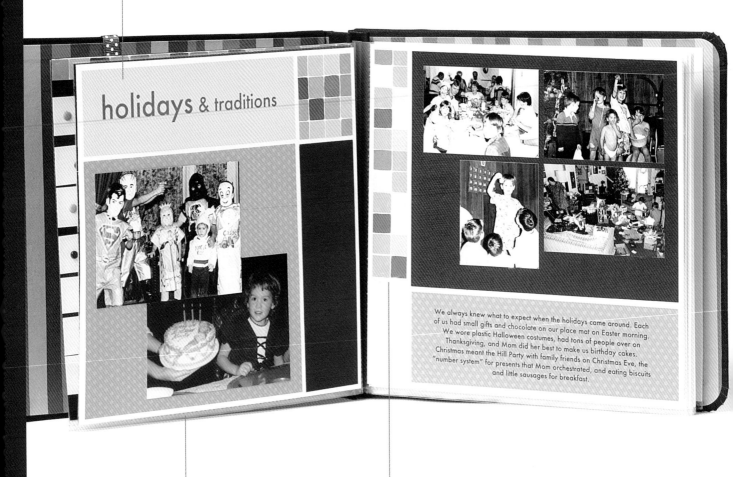

holidays & traditions

We always knew what to expect when the holidays came around. Each of us had small gifts and chocolate on our place mat on Easter morning. We wore plastic Halloween costumes, had tons of people over on Thanksgiving, and Mom did her best to make us birthday cakes. Christmas meant the Hill Party with family friends on Christmas Eve, the "number system" for presents that Mom orchestrated, and eating biscuits and little sausages for breakfast.

{ **3: DESIGN** }

Select a fun and vibrant color scheme to make your album appealing to children.

{ **2: ORGANIZE** }

Add a table of contents to the front of your album for easy reference.

Don't be shy about including "imperfect" photographs from your childhood on your pages.

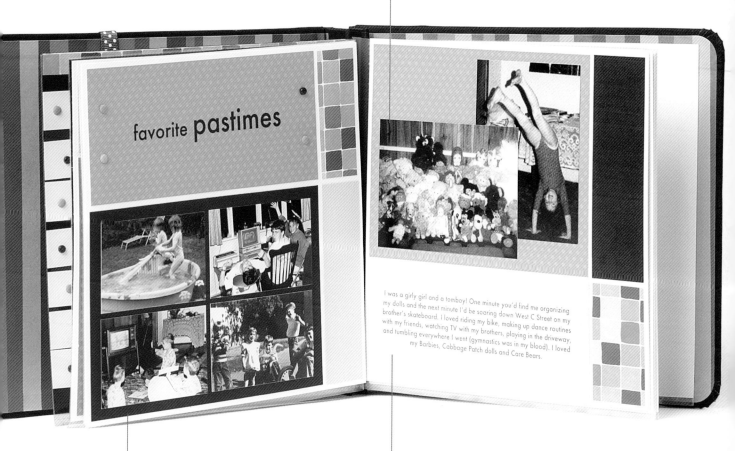

I was a girly girl and a tomboy! One minute you'd find me organizing my dolls and the next minute I'd be soaring down West C Street on my brother's skateboard. I loved riding my bike, making up dance routines with my friends, watching TV with my brothers, playing in the driveway, and tumbling everywhere I went (gymnastics was in my blood). I loved my Barbies, Cabbage Patch dolls and Care Bears.

{ 5: JOURNAL }

Share details about your "favorites" in your journaling.

{ 6: REMEMBER }

It's okay to create a summary of your childhood—you don't have to document each year!

at your age

1968, tipp city

1971 mennison

1974 with robin, tell...from...

I loved to look through clothes catalogs. I went through a dress-only phase. I would cry if my parents looked at me cross-eyed. I had a puppy that broke it's leg. I did not talk much. I was a lot like you.

I hated bumps in my socks. I learned to read before I started kindergarten. I had a puppy who ate my favorite pair of pants. I learned how to ride a two-wheeler. I was a lot like you.

I was terrified of killer bees. I became nervous when asked to try anything new. I got caught calling a boy on the phone. I had lived in 3 different cities. I loved to explore the creek near our house. I loved to swim. I read all the time. I was a lot like you.

journaled february 2005

Be Inspired

At Your Age *by* Rhonda Stark

Supplies *Software:* Adobe Photoshop; *Papers and ribbon:* Gina Cabrera, digitaldesignessentials.com; *Computer fonts:* AL Charles "Essentials" CD and A: Constitution, "Vintage" CD, Autumn Leaves.

Becky's album inspired me to:

Compare and contrast my childhood likes and dislikes with my daughter's.

Record a couple of my favorite family stories on a layout.

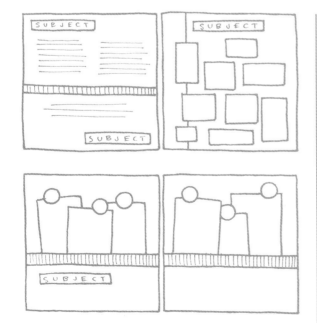

Scrapbook Yourself Today

If something were to happen to me, I'd want my children to know as much about me as they possibly can. I created this album as a visual inventory of who I am today.

Supplies *Album, patterned paper, foam stamps, slide and eyelets:* Making Memories; *Ribbon:* May Arts and Making Memories; *Letter stamp:* Li'l Davis Designs; *Negative strips:* Creative Imaginations; *Circle punch:* Family Treasures; *Flat-top eyelets:* Doodlebug Design; *Computer fonts:* CK Postage Due and CK True Type, "The Heritage, Vintage & Retro Collection" CD, *Creating Keepsakes;* Century Gothic, downloaded from the Internet.

Make a list of what you want your children to know about you.

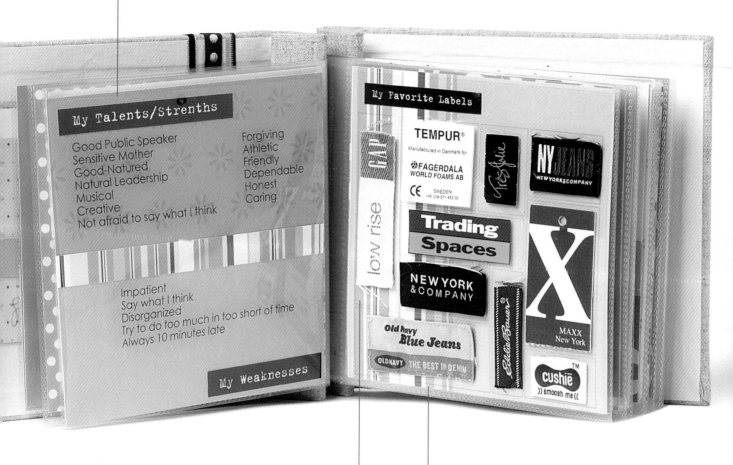

My Talents/Strenths

Good Public Speaker
Sensitive Mother
Good-Natured
Natural Leadership
Musical
Creative
Not afraid to say what I think

Forgiving
Athletic
Friendly
Dependable
Honest
Caring

Impatient
Say what I think
Disorganized
Try to do too much in too short of time
Always 10 minutes late

My Weaknesses

My Favorite Labels

TEMPUR®
Manufactured in Denmark for
FAGERDALA
WORLD FOAMS AB
CE SWEDEN
+46 (0)8-571 452 00

Très Jolie

NY JEANS
NEW YORK & COMPANY

Trading
Spaces

X
MAXX
New York

NEW YORK
& COMPANY

Eddie Bauer

Old Navy
Blue Jeans

OLD NAVY THE BEST IN DENIM

cushie
)) smoosh me ((

Personalize your page design with business cards, price tags and even receipts from your favorite store.

Take a creative approach—make a layout based around tags from a favorite clothing item.

*Slip handwritten letters to your children
into a page pocket.*

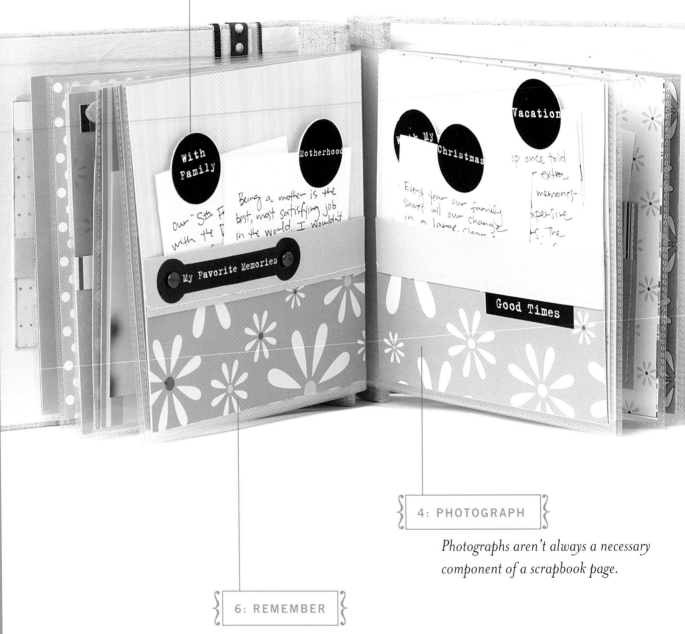

4: PHOTOGRAPH

*Photographs aren't always a necessary
component of a scrapbook page.*

6: REMEMBER

*It's important to scrapbook about yourself—your
family will love discovering more about you.*

SIMPLY ME

THE Good

Spunky, fun, *spontaneous*, generous, kind, joker, *playful*, creative.

THE Bad

clumsy, forgetful, flakey, *messy*, unorganized, to much of a *sweet tooth*, horrible cook!

THE Favorites

Chocolate, 80's music, my kids, McDonald's, *my camera*, scrapbook supplies, *Angel's voice*, my garage, Survivor

Be Inspired

Simply Me *by* Suzy West

Supplies *Textured cardstock:* Bazzill Basics Paper; *Patterned paper:* Chatterbox; *Letter stencils:* Making Memories; *Wood letters:* Li'l Davis Designs; *Plastic letters:* Westrim Crafts; *Ribbon:* C.M. Offray & Son; *Label maker:* Dymo; *Stamping ink:* Nick Bantock, Ranger Industries; *Other:* Flower.

Lisa's album inspired me to:

● Realize that my family will enjoy reading about who I am.

● Write journaling that uses just a few words to convey my personality.

10 Ideas for Scrapbooking Your Dreams

AS SCRAPBOOKERS, we often create pages about the memories of our past. We sometimes create pages that are a snapshot of our present. But, it can also be fun to scrapbook our dreams of the future. These 10 tips will help you get started scrapbooking your dreams (and perhaps making them come true!).

- Describe your dream home. Do you dream about renovating an old Victorian home with a wrap-around porch and gables, or is your dream home a two-story colonial with columns and a swimming pool?

- Schedule the perfect day in your life. If you had unlimited funds, how would you spend the next 24 hours?

- What's your perfect career? Do you dream of being in a helping occupation, such as a nurse, a teacher or a social worker? Or, do you dream of a job in a creative industry such as a writer, artist, designer or musician?

- If you could do just one thing to make the world a better place, what would it be and why?

- Create a travelogue that documents your dream vacation. Where would you go and why?

- If you won a million dollars, how would you spend it?

- If you could spend a day with one person, who would it be? What would you hope to learn from spending the day with this person?

- Make a list of books you want to read and movies you want to watch this year.

- What's your dream car? Do you like a powerful engine or a sleek sporty look?

- If you could take a class on any subject (for free!), what would it be? Where would you travel to take the class?

More About Me

ALBUM 16

by Becky Higgins

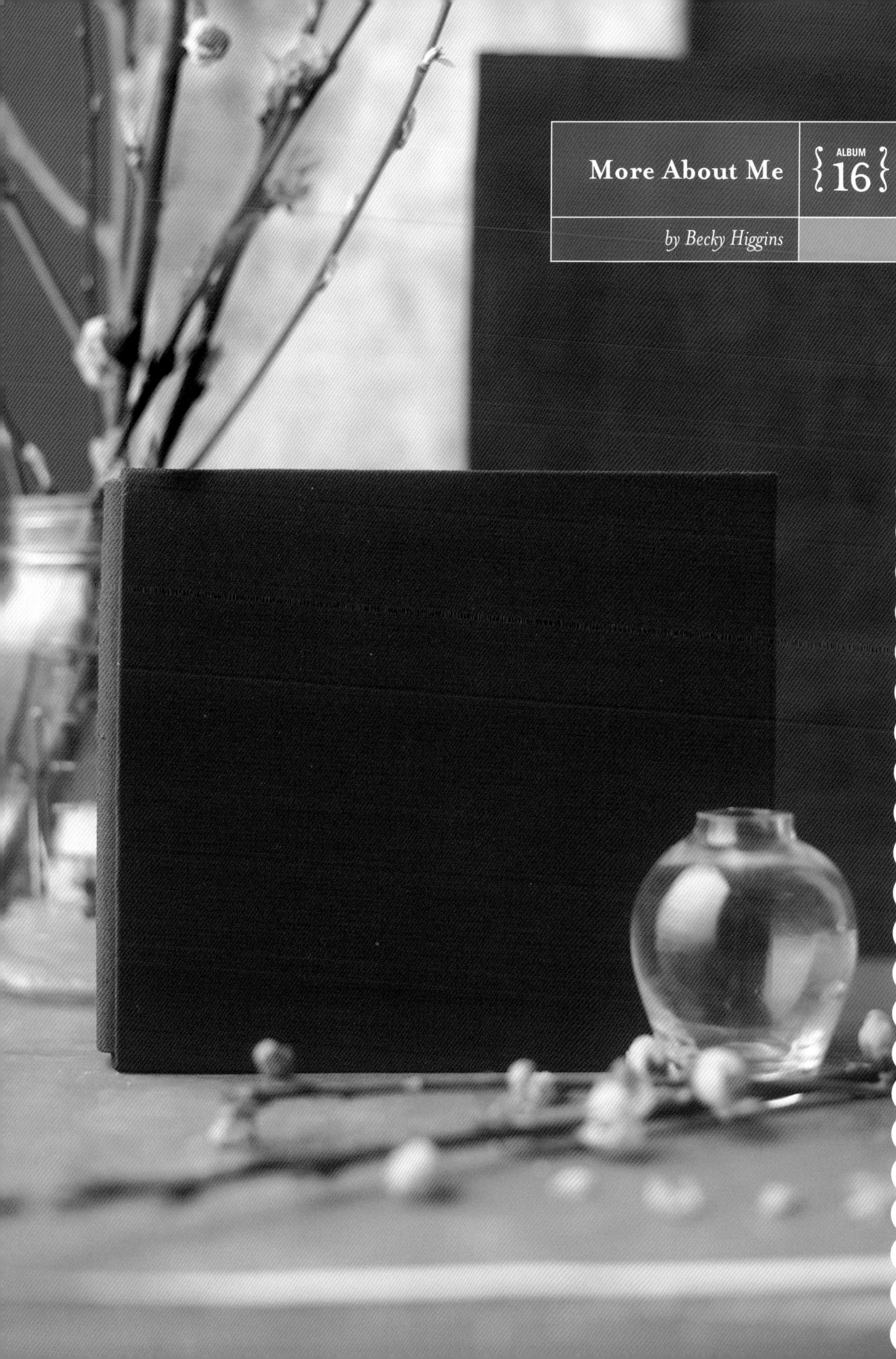

A Brief Autobiography

This album is a brief autobiography, a way for me to sum up my life in just a few pages. The first half of this album shows the top 10 loves of my life. The second half, part of which is shown here, is a brief history of my life.

Supplies *Album:* Making Memories; *Patterned papers:* Design Originals (dictionary), The Paper Loft (red); *Foam Stamps:* Making Memories; *Acrylic paint:* Delta Technical Coatings; *Computer fonts:* Century Gothic (journaling), Microsoft Word; Unknown ("More About Me"); *Photo corners:* Canson; *Brads:* Magic Scraps; *Other:* Stitching.

*Make a list of journaling topics for
your autobiography.*

*Set up a journaling template on
your computer and type sentences
on each topic.*

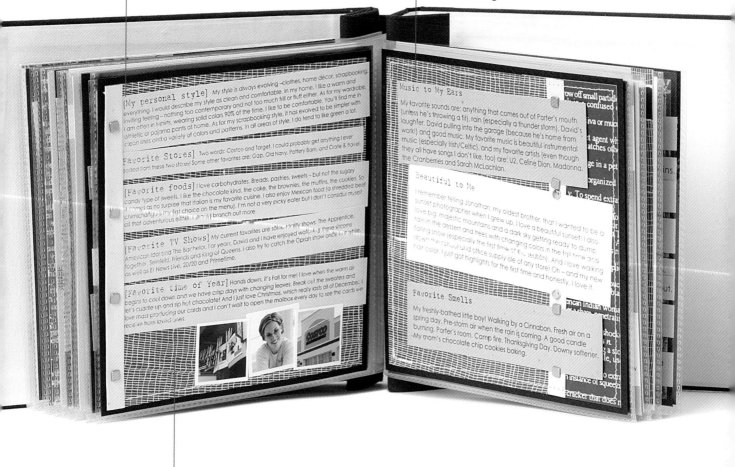

*Print your journaling, cut it into strips and
arrange it on your page layouts.*

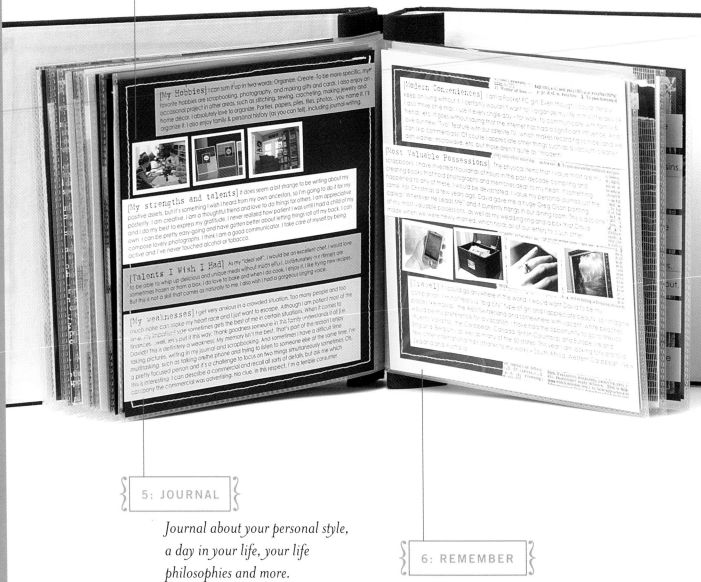

4: PHOTOGRAPH

Use index prints as page–design elements.

5: JOURNAL

Journal about your personal style, a day in your life, your life philosophies and more.

6: REMEMBER

This is your autobiography—you can share as much or as little as you'd like!

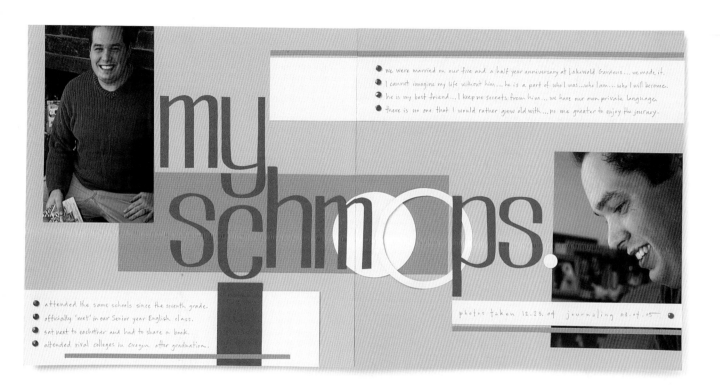

we were married on our five and a half year anniversary at Lakewold Gardens... we made it.

I cannot imagine my life without him... he is a part of who I was... who I am... who I will become.

he is my best friend... I keep no secrets from him... we have our own private language.

there is no one that I would rather grow old with... no one greater to enjoy the journey.

attended the same schools since the seventh grade.

officially 'met' in our Senior year English class.

sat next to eachother and had to share a book.

attended rival colleges in Oregon after graduation.

photos taken 12.23.04   journaling 03.04.05

Be Inspired

My Schmops *by* Carrie Owen

Supplies *Textured cardstock:* Bazzill Basics Paper; *Title and journaling:* Carrie's own writing; *Pen:* Zig Writer, EK Success; *Other:* Studs.

Becky's album inspired me to:

Journal my thoughts and feelings about my husband on paper strips.

Record the "all about us" story of how I met and fell in love with my husband.

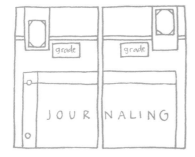

Scrapbook Those School Photos

I inherited my husband's school photos and needed an easy way to get them into an album so they can be compared, contrasted and, most importantly, enjoyed.

Supplies *Album:* Westrim Crafts; *Textured cardstock:* Bazzill Basics Paper; *Patterned papers:* Daisy D's Paper Co. (cracked), The Paper Loft (rustic letters), Karen Foster Design (notebook) and 7gypsies (skinny letters); *Photo corners:* Canson; *Foam stamps and acrylic paint:* Making Memories; *Corner rounder:* Marvy Uchida; *Bookplate:* Li'l Davis Designs; *Brads:* Making Memories; *Computer fonts:* Century Schoolbook BT and Skia, downloaded from the Internet.

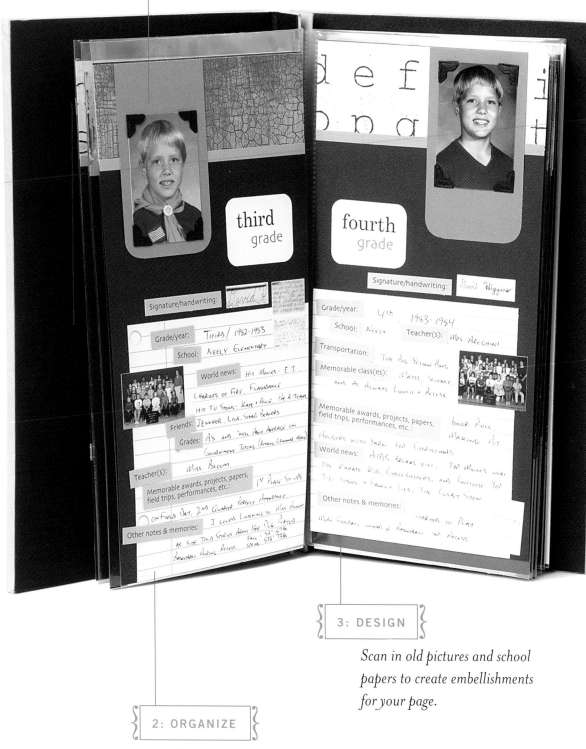

1: PREPARE

Gather school photographs and memorabilia.

3: DESIGN

Scan in old pictures and school papers to create embellishments for your page.

2: ORGANIZE

Create one page for each school year, adding a photograph and written memories for that year.

You probably won't remember every single detail from your school days—record the moments that stand out in your mind.

4: PHOTOGRAPH

Look at ID cards, yearbooks pages and school newspaper articles for additional photos to feature on your page.

5: JOURNAL

Print out a variety of journaling prompts to help you recall your school memories.

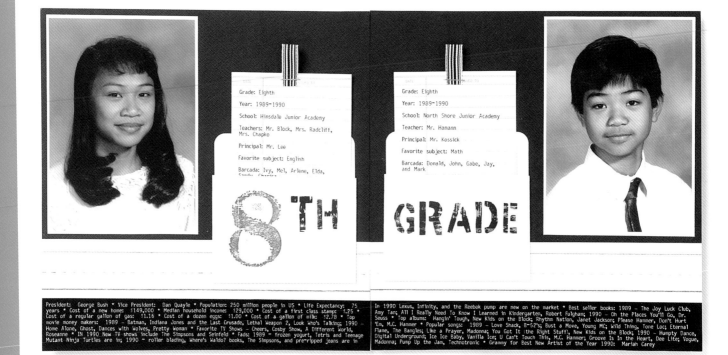

Grade: Eighth

Year: 1989-1990

School: Hinsdale Junior Academy

Teachers: Mr. Block, Mrs. Radcliff, Mrs. Chapko

Principal: Mr. Lee

Favorite subject: English

Barcada: Ivy, Mel, Arlene, Elda, Sandy, Cherica

Grade: Eighth

Year: 1989-1990

School: North Shore Junior Academy

Teacher: Mr. Hamann

Principal: Mr. Kossick

Favorite subject: Math

Barcada: Donald, John, Gabe, Jay, and Mark

8TH GRADE

President: George Bush * Vice President: Dan Quayle * Population: 250 million people in US * Life Expectancy: 75 years * Cost of a new home: $149,000 * Median household income: $29,000 * Cost of a first class stamp: $.25 * Cost of a regular gallon of gas: $1.16 * Cost of a dozen eggs: $1.00 * Cost of a gallon of milk: $2.78 * Top movie money makers: 1989 - Batman, Indiana Jones and the Last Crusade, Lethal Weapon 2, Look Who's Talking; 1990 - Home Alone, Ghost, Dances with Wolves, Pretty Woman * Favorite TV Shows - Cheers, Cosby Show, A Different World, Roseanne * IN 1990 New TV shows include The Simpsons and Seinfeld * Fads: 1989 - frozen yogurt, Tetris and Teenage Mutant Ninja Turtles are in; 1990 - roller blading, Where's Waldo? books, The Simpsons, and pre-ripped jeans are in

In 1990 Lexus, Infinity, and the Reebok pump are new on the market * Best seller books: 1989 - The Joy Luck Club, Amy Tan; All I Really Need To Know I Learned in Kindergarten, Robert Fulgham; 1990 - Oh the Places You'll Go, Dr. Seuss * Top albums: Hangin' Tough, New Kids on the Block; Rhythm Nation, Janet Jackson; Please Hammer, Don't Hurt 'Em, M.C. Hammer * Popular songs: 1989 - Love Shack, B-52's; Bust a Move, Young MC; Wild Thing, Tone Loc; Eternal Flame, The Bangles; Like a Prayer, Madonna; You Got It (the Right Stuff), New Kids on the Block; 1990 - Humpty Dance, Digital Underground; Ice Ice Baby, Vanilla Ice; U Can't Touch This, M.C. Hammer; Groove Is In the Heart, Dee Lite; Vogue, Madonna; Pump Up the Jam, Technotronic * Grammy for Best New Artist of the Year 1990: Mariah Carey

Be Inspired

8th Grade *by* Joy Uzarraga

Supplies *Textured cardstock:* Bazzill Basics Paper; *Patterned paper:* Creative Imaginations; *Letter stickers:* Art Warehouse, Creative Imaginations; *Number stamp:* Art Warehouse for Limited Edition Rubberstamps; *Stamping ink:* Ancient Page, Clearsnap; *Library cards and pockets:* Boxer Scrapbook Productions; *Ribbon:* May Arts; *Computer font:* Carbonated Gothic, downloaded from the Internet; *Other:* Staples.

Becky's album inspired me to:

Create a layout that compared and contrasted my eighth grade experience with my husband's.

Take the time to scrapbook my school photographs (I'd really hate for them to get lost!).

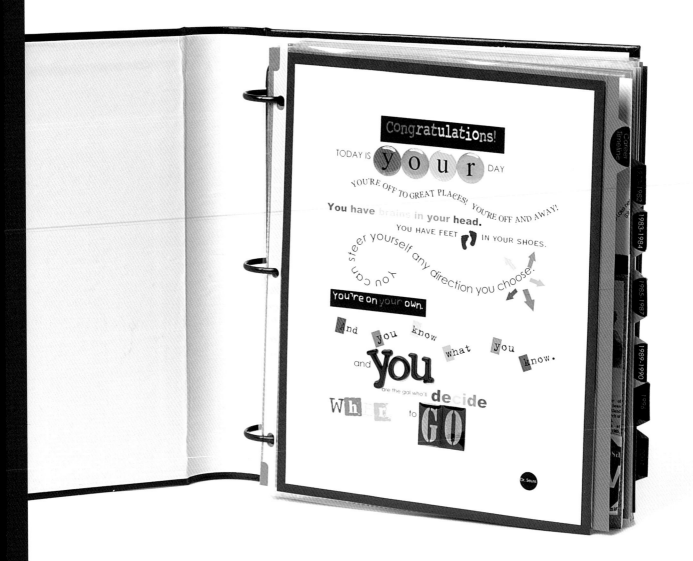

Create a Visual Resume

My career is a big part of who I am. When I created this album, I thought it would be fun to share my career timeline with my family. Instead of writing long paragraphs of information, I decided to create a visual timeline that can be understood at a glance.

Supplies *Album:* Target; *Patterned paper:* Design Originals; *Letter stamps:* Postmodern Design and River City Rubber Stamps; *Stamping ink:* ColorBox, Clearsnap; *Letter stickers:* Making Memories and KI Memories; *Epoxy letters:* Li'l Davis Designs; *Foot punch:* Marvy Uchida; *Bookplate and brads:* Making Memories; *Tack:* K&Company; *Computer fonts:* Century Gothic, downloaded from the Internet; CK Newsman, CK True Type, CK True Type Distressed, CK Postage Due, and CK Stenography, "The Heritage, Vintage & Retro Collection" CD; CK Twilight, CK Corral and CK Carbon Copy, "Fresh Fonts" CD; CK Regal, "Creative Clips & Fonts for Special Occasions" CD, *Creating Keepsakes;* Arial Black, Microsoft Word; *Other:* Cork paper.

Sketch out a timeline that shows various jobs you've held in your life.

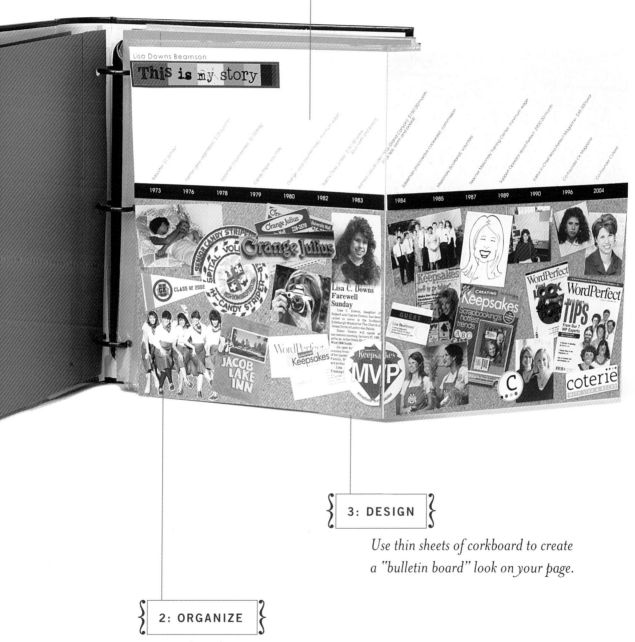

3: DESIGN

Use thin sheets of corkboard to create a "bulletin board" look on your page.

2: ORGANIZE

Scan photographs, business cards, magazine covers and more to illustrate your timeline.

Just a few details (about your job title and salary) will help tell your career story.

{ 4: PHOTOGRAPH }

Add photographs of yourself at different life stages to help tell the story of how you've changed and grown.

{ 6: REMEMBER }

Inspiration is all around us— this album was inspired by an Ellison press kit!

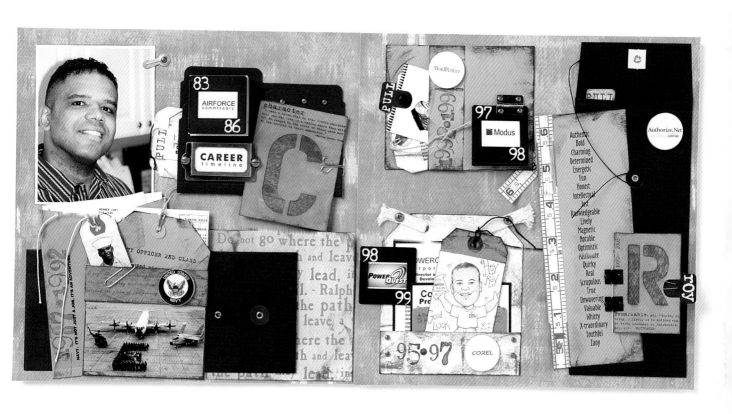

Be Inspired

Career Timeline *by* Kristy Banks

Supplies *Patterned papers:* Rusty Pickle, Rocky Mountain Scrapbook Company, Karen Foster Design and Pixie Press; *Letter stamps:* Postmodern Design; *Slide mounts:* Loersch; *Envelopes and chipboard circles:* Bazzill Basics Paper; *Stamping ink:* Ranger Industries; *Bookplate:* Li'l Davis Designs; *Tags and file folders:* Rusty Pickle; *Rub-ons, brads, screw eyelets, hinges, date stamp, letter stamps, brown envelope, cards and tag:* Making Memories; *Photo anchor:* 7gypsies; *Stencils:* Autumn Leaves; *Circle punch:* Family Treasures; *Vintage tabs:* Melissa Frances; *Large tag:* K&Company; *Computer fonts:* Arial, Arial Black, Futura MD, Arial Narrow, Microsoft Word; CK True Type, "The Heritage, Vintage & Retro Collection" CD and LB Sandbox, "Lisa's Favorite Fonts" CD, *Creating Keepsakes;* OZ Handicraft, downloaded from the Internet.

Lisa's album inspired me to:

Create a layout that documents my husband's career path, work ethic and personality traits.

Tuck little stories into hidden pockets on my layout (I know my children will be delighted to discover these extra stories about their dad!).

Signature/handwriting: David H.

Grade/year: Third / 1952-1953

School: Neely Elementary

World news: Hit Movies - E.T.
Chariots of Fire, Flashdance
Hit T.V. Shows - Kate & Allie, the A-Te

Friends: Jennifer, Lisa, Shad Beavers

Grades: A's and "well above average on
Government Testing (Reading, Grammar, M

Teacher(s): Miss Bloom

Memorable awards, projects, papers,
field trips, performances, etc.: 1st Place St...

Other notes & memories: On Field Day, 2nd Quarter Perfect Attendance.
I loved Listening to Miss Bloom
as she told stories about how Dog Played
Fall - 53°° 67th ...
Spring - 538 73th

With Family

Motherhood

Our "5th F...
with the D...

Being a mother is the
best, most satisfying job
in the world. I wouldn't...

My Favorite Memories

*Add surprises to your layouts
by tucking notes into pockets
and adding handwritten letters
and tiny photographs to
mini-albums on your pages.*

MEMBER COPY
514 /03A

TY OFFICER 2ND CLASS

UNITED STATES
NAVY

NAVY, IT'S NOT JUST A JOB...

*Share "imperfect" photographs
from your childhood and
allow your children to delight
in finding details in photographs
such as floppy disk drives and
panelled walls.*

5

~

cherish

~

Pass along your family traditions
with cherished stories
that define your values.

Porter Wayne Higgins, the First Year

by Becky Higgins

Baby's First Year, Fast

It's a challenge being a new mom! I wanted to create a non-overwhelming way to scrapbook my son's first-year photographs. This simple "picture album" is designed as a quick overview of Porter's growth during his first year. I saved the more detailed journaling and photos for a larger scrapbook.

Supplies *Album, ribbon, frame, epoxy stickers, brads and bookplate:* Making Memories; *Patterned paper:* Chatterbox; *Computer fonts:* Hootie!, downloaded from *www.free-typewriter-fonts.com*; Century Gothic, Microsoft Word.

A picture-book format will allow you to easily share your layouts with your child.

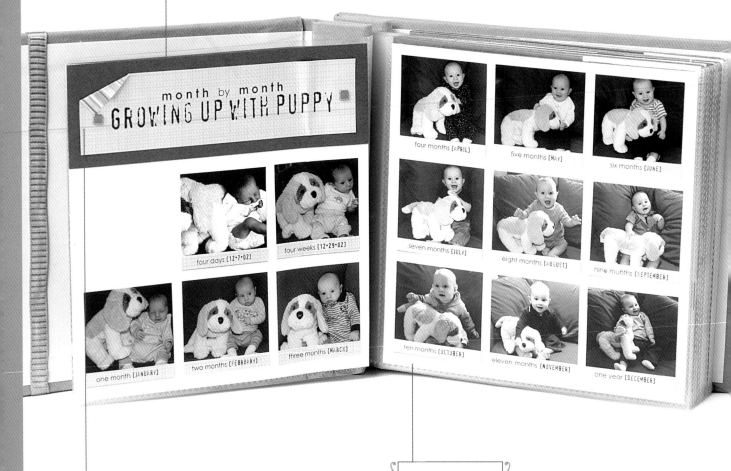

1: PREPARE

Take photographs of your child with a favorite stuffed toy to show growth progression.

3: DESIGN

Fold back corners of double-sided paper or crumple paper tags to add visual interest to pages.

Collect two favorite photographs from each month of your child's first year.

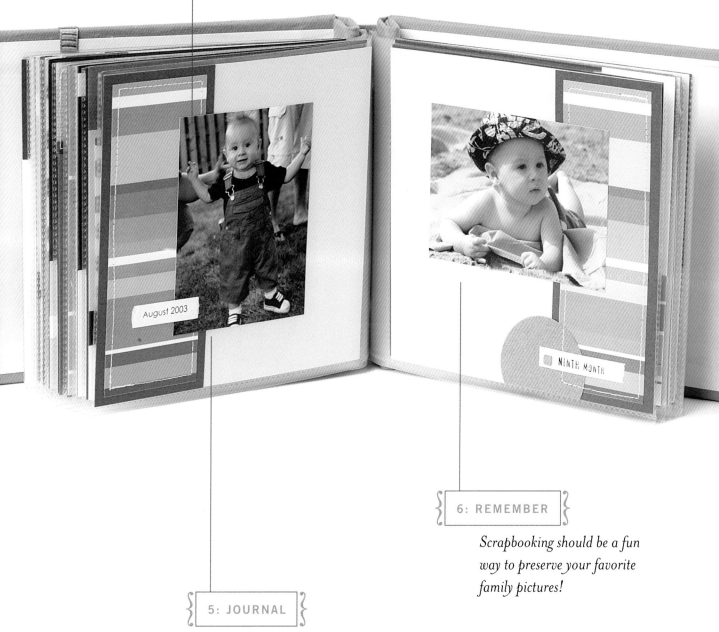

August 2003

NINTH MONTH

Scrapbooking should be a fun way to preserve your favorite family pictures!

These photographs tell stories without words (notice Porter standing at nine months!)

Be Inspired

To show you how easily you can transfer an album layout to a scrapbook-page layout, I re-created the story of photographing Porter with the puppy on a 12" x 12" spread.

On the spread, I can include the journaling details I left out of the album. My journaling reads, *"It all started in the Fall of 2002. A couple of months before Porter was born, my mom and I spent a day in Frazeysburg, Ohio, at the Longaberger Homestead … it was there that I found this stuffed animal and bought it for our son-to-be. I took a picture of Porter with Puppy when he was just five days old and then a couple weeks old … and so forth. As he got older, Porter looked for Puppy each time we put him in his crib and snuggled with him as he slept. So here it is — a glance of Porter's growth his first year … with Puppy."*

Supplies *Textured cardstock:* Bazzill Basics Paper; *Pattered paper:* American Crafts; *Letter and number stickers:* Doodlebug Designs; *Pen:* Zig Millennium, EK Success; *Computer fonts:* CK Toggle, "The Best Of Creative Lettering" CD Vol. 2, Creating Keepsakes.

Successful marriages and families are established and maintained on principles of

faith prayer
repentance
forgiveness
respect love
COMPASSION
WORK
and
wholesome
recreational activities

Proclamation to the World
The Church of Jesus Christ of Latter-Day Saints

name and attributes

Scrapbook Your Values

My starting place for this book was a statement from my church about marriage and families, a proclamation that is at the core of my belief system. I took words from the statement, like faith, respect, and love, and created pages about people I know who exemplify each value.

Supplies *Album, patterned paper, stickers and binder:* SEI; *Ribbon:* May Arts; *Computer fonts:* CK Fraternity, Becky Higgins' "Creative Clips & Fonts" CD; CK Hot Rod, CK Gershwin and CK Retro Block, "The Heritage, Vintage & Retro Collection" CD; CK Handprint, "The Best of Creative Lettering" CD Combo; CK Newsprint and CK Chemistry, "Fresh Fonts" CD; CK Tween, "Creative Clips & Fonts for Girls" CD, *Creating Keepsakes*; Typewriter and Century Gothic, downloaded from the Internet.

Start with an inspirational passage from a favorite book or poem.

Since the time I was young, my mom has invited many people to live in our home. She calls them her "adopted children" and they call her mom.

These people come from all walks of life and from different countries around the world. It seems at every holiday celebration, there are twice as many people because of this huge extended family.

My mom can talk to anyone no matter the language barrier. She makes everyone feel as if she's known them for years. My mom truly respects every person for who they are—she loves every color, shape and size of all mankind.

Who Clarine Kiehl Downs
Where Orem, Utah
When Her adult life
respect

Gwen Bearnson McNamara
Riverton, Utah
1989- 2005
love

From the moment I first met Steve's sister, Gwen, I knew there was something special about her. She was so sweet to me the moment I met her and made me feel welcome in their family.

Since that time, I've discovered what makes Gwen so great. She truly loves people! She is the only aunt on either side of the family who always remembers birthdays. We all look forward to that birthday call from Gwen. She also makes wonderful homemade gifts. One year she sewed a blanket for every cousin in the family, another year hand-beaded bracelets for all the girls.

3: DESIGN

Choose a two-color design scheme that can be repeated on each page.

2: ORGANIZE

Select words from the passage and make a list of people who emulate each word.

For a fun twist on this album, create a book based on one value that defines who you are.

4: PHOTOGRAPH

I decided to feature black-and-white photographs in my album for a unified look.

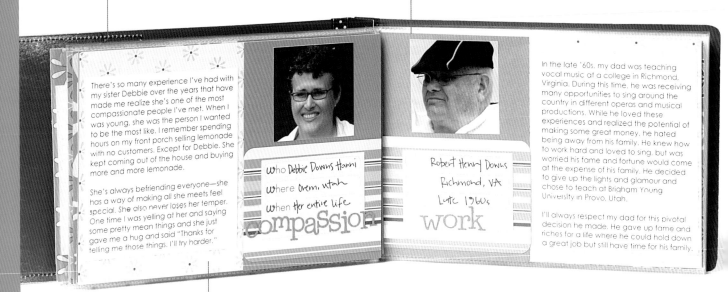

There's so many experience I've had with my sister Debbie over the years that have made me realize she's one of the most compassionate people I've met. When I was young, she was the person I wanted to be the most like. I remember spending hours on my front porch selling lemonade with no customers. Except for Debbie. She kept coming out of the house and buying more and more lemonade.

She's always befriending everyone—she has a way of making all she meets feel special. She also never loses her temper. One time I was yelling at her and saying some pretty mean things and she just gave me a hug and said "Thanks for telling me those things. I'll try harder."

Who Debbie Downs Hanni
Where Orem, Utah
When Her entire life
compassion

Robert Henry Downs
Richmond, VA
Late 1960s
work

In the late '60s, my dad was teaching vocal music at a college in Richmond, Virginia. During this time, he was receiving many opportunities to sing around the country in different operas and musical productions. While he loved these experiences and realized the potential of making some great money, he hated being away from his family. He knew how to work hard and loved to sing, but was worried his fame and fortune would come at the expense of his family. He decided to give up the lights and glamour and chose to teach at Brigham Young University in Provo, Utah.

I'll always respect my dad for this pivotal decision he made. He gave up fame and riches for a life where he could hold down a great job but still have time for his family.

6: REMEMBER

Scrapbooking your personal value system is a great way to reaffirm who you are.

Be Inspired

The Infinite Worth of a Woman

by Sunny Kohler

Supplies *Patterned paper:* 7gypsies; *Foam stamps, metal word, ribbon charm and acrylic paint:* Making Memories; *Metal accents:* Karen Foster Design; *Stamping ink:* Hero Arts; *Computer fonts:* CK Elegant, CK Constitution and CK Chemistry, "Fresh Fonts" CD, *Creating Keepsakes*.

Lisa's album inspired me to:

Teach my children about their heritage.

Cherish the knowledge that I come from a strong line of women who had hopes, dreams and strong values.

Treasures of the Heart

Expensive things really aren't important to me. I once had a pricey wedding ring and it was flushed down the toilet or put in a heater vent by one of my small boys. After a day of searching, another day of tears and yet another day of scoldings, I soon got over the lose. I realized that people are worth more than things and felt thankful that my family was well and happy. You can't take "things" with you in the next life, but relationships will last forever.

Since that day, I've collected many treasures. They aren't gold, or silver, or even another wedding ring (the ring I wear is $40.00). In fact, if a thief broke into my home, most likely these possessions would be passed by. My treasures are those items that are priceless to my heart.

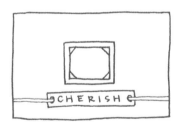

A Collection of Treasures

When I created this album, I wanted a book where I could display the treasures of my heart. These are items that a thief would never take from my home but that are precious to me nonetheless.

Supplies *Mini album, ribbon, "Cherish" on cover and ribbon letter charms:* Making Memories; *Computer fonts:* Source unknown; *Stamping ink:* Ranger Industries.

{ 1: PREPARE }

Make a list of items that are precious to you.

{ 2: ORGANIZE }

Photograph each item (or ask your child to draw a picture of it for you!).

Collin's Glasses

Every time I see these glasses, a little giggle escapes my mouth. When Collin was six, he insisted he needed glasses. I took him to the eye doctor and after a thorough exam determined that Collin's eye sight was perfect–no glasses needed. For the next year, Collin complained about not being able to see the chalkboard at school and that he was going to get bad grades because of this condition.

He finally convinced me to take him to the doctor again. After another thorough exam, he sent Collin to the waiting room and said: "For some reason your son thinks he needs glasses but his vision is perfect. Here's a prescription for glasses that have only clear glass in them–that will solve the problem." I later asked Collin why he wanted glasses. "Because Chelsea wears them," he wailed. Collin got the glasses and faithfully wore them. I'm happy to say there was no more complaining and no more bad grades. Collin was 10 before he learned the truth about these glasses. They reminds me there's a solution to every problem and to find humor in all situations of life.

every moment holds a hidden **gift**.

{ 3: DESIGN }

Choose a theme for the album (a heart theme would be a fun way to showcase what you love!).

Use your zoom lens to take macro shots of your cherished items.

Heart-Shaped Rock

"Mom, I have a big surprise for you." I can still hear the excitement in Brecken's voice as I recall these words. She made me close my eyes, then put something hard with a pointed edge in my hand. "It's a heart-shaped rock," she exclaimed. "I found it outside and wanted to give it to you so you'll always remember how much you and dad love each other."

This rock sits front and center on my dresser. I see it several times a day. It's a wonderful reminder in life's hectic world that my relationship with Steve is really the most important relationship of all. Thanks to a 6-year-old girl for this priceless gift.

Happy are the Pure in heart

{ 5: JOURNAL }

Tell the story about why you treasure each item in your album.

{ 6: REMEMBER }

A treasure can be anything you want it to be: a note from a friend, a smile from a stranger, a conversation that makes you laugh.

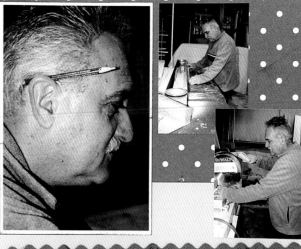

I can't remember a time when I did not see a pencil on my Dad's ear. Whenever you needed to jot something down or needed to make a quick note you knew that Dad always had a pencil on his ear. Now that I am older and have a Son of my own I know that the little piece of wood on my Father's ear was not only a pencil but an expression of who he was, and has become. It is a great Artistic extension of the Man he is today. My Father is a Michelangelo when it comes to wood. You can start to describe what you would like and he grabs for his pencil and draws it out just as you imagined, if not better. This little pencil that I have taken for granted all my life as just a tool to help make my life a little easier was really a wonderful treasure to me. Every time I look at a pencil I think of my Dad working at his shop, the sound of the band saw, the smell of freshly cut wood, the lacquer from the spray booth, playing in the sawdust, or running our fingers around the belt sander and always getting them pinched after Dad told us we would. I still remember when we would get to help sweep up for the night, we thought we were the luckiest kids in the whole world. He always made you feel like you were important and what you were doing was important. Even if it was work, we thought we were lucky to be with our Dad. My Dad worked in a cabinet shop connected to our home until I was around the age of 18 years old (1998). So coming home from school and running in to the house having a snack that Mom had on the counter for us everyday, and running in to say hi to my Dad was a daily routine for us. Looking forward to seeing my parents after school, I had the best of both worlds. Mom being a wonderful Woman, staying home, and being a room Mother every year to all FIVE of her children. My Father was often at home when other Dad's were at work. Even though Dad worked at home he was gone a lot, but Mom would have dinner ready for him on the table when he came home. I have such a great respect for my Dad. In all the years that he has worked, he never worked on Sunday. He would work on Christmas after the presents had been opened but keeping the Sabbath day holy was very important to him and he has passed that down to us. Some Dads do computers, some Dads do sports, but my Dad has left a legacy and doesn't even know it all from one little pencil that is kept behind his ear. Now the legacy lives on through his Sons, and Grandsons of putting a pencil behind their ears, which will fill their families with wonderful memories, all from a little piece of wood.

Be Inspired

Treasures of the Heart *by* Alison Marquis

Supplies *Textured cardstock:* DieCuts with a View; *Patterned paper:* Making Memories; *Monogram:* My Mind's Eye; *Tag:* Doodlebug Design; *Stamping ink:* Memories, Stewart Superior Corporation; *Ribbon:* Dashes, Dots, and Checks; *Computer font:* Broadcast, downloaded from the Internet.

Lisa's album inspired me to:

Record the special story about my dad's habit

of always keeping a pencil behind his ear.

Think about all the things I love about

my dad.

10 Stories to Share on a Page

AS SCRAPBOOKERS, we all have stories to tell, but sometimes it's hard to find a starting point. Here is a list of 10 stories you might want to tell on a scrapbook page (maybe one of them will inspire you to remember a story you've forgotten!).

Tell a story about a time when you …

- Failed a test. How did you feel? What did you learn from the experience?

- Set a goal and reached it. How did you reach your goal? How long did it take?

- Played in the rain or the snow as a child. How have your feelings about the weather changed over the years?

- Received an unexpected gift from a friend. How did it make you feel? How did you thank him or her?

- Had an accident. What happened? How did it change your life?

- Decided to change your mind about something important. What was it? Do you reject your decision to change your mind?

- Changed your look. What did you change? How did people react?

- Regretted saying something. What did you say? What would you have said differently?

- Wished a day would never end. Why was the day special?

- Drove someplace you'd never been before. Where did you go? Did you get lost?

Favorite Dates Folio

Although this isn't a "traditional" album, it's a project that's very close to my heart! This folio is a place where I've collected snippets that represent my favorite date nights with my husband, Steve.

Supplies *Album:* Bazzill Basics Paper; *Patterned paper:* Source unknown; *Tags and binding tape:* Making Memories; *Letter stickers:* American Crafts; *Acrylic letters:* Doodlebug Design; *Ribbon:* May Arts; *Music charm:* Buttons Galore; *Dimensional adhesive:* Diamond Glaze, JudiKins.

*Start with a portfolio (this one is designed
for displaying a coin collection).*

2 : ORGANIZE

*Collect business cards, brochures, tickets, napkins and
more from the places you go on dates.*

Steve and I look forward to "Date Night" every week. Whether we are alone or with a group of friends, we seem to have fun with whatever we're doing. Here are "snippets" of some of our favorite places to go or things to do.
Restaurants: Buca di Beppo, IHop (breakfast dates are the best), Tepanyaki, Chilis and California Pizza Kitchen (the whole wheat crust on their pizza is the best). **Games**: Phase 10 (also Lucky Unders with these cards), Fact or Crap, Apples to Apples, Rook and Nertz. **Sporting Events:** BYU basketball and football games, Jazz basketball, bowling and raquetball. **Other stuff:** concerts, shopping at REI to get sporting goods, bike rides, listening to KSL radio in the car and movies (always with a big bucket of popcorn and peanut M&Ms).

{ 3: DESIGN }

Use a coin as a template to size
your date-night memorabilia.

{ 4: REMEMBER }

Memories can be preserved in
a variety of creative ways!

Wow! 17 years! It seems like Terry and I have been married forever, but then again those 17 years have flown by. Our 3-day anniversary get-away that Terry planned was just what I needed to rejuvenate my soul. There is no one else I'd rather LAUGH with, play with, or SHARE my life with. Sometimes I WONDER what my life would have been like without him. But then again, I can't imagine living life without him. He is my SOUL MATE!

always and FOREVER

Be Inspired

Together 17 Years *by* Angela Ash

Supplies *Patterned papers:* Chatterbox (navy and flower) and BasicGrey (light blue); *Foam stamps, acrylic paint, tin tiles, ribbon charm, brads and definitions:* Making Memories; *Letter stamps:* PSX Design and Stampin' Up!; *Word stamps:* 7gypsies; *"Love" tabs:* Autumn Leaves; *Library pockets:* Bazzill Basics Paper; *Stamping ink:* Ranger Industries and Tsukineko; *Clock stamps:* Impression Obsession (large) and Making Memories (small); *Charms:* Darice (snowflake) and All My Memories "forever"; *Computer font:* Antique Type, downloaded from the Internet; *Other:* Date stamp, label maker and fibers.

Lisa's decorated folio inspired me to:

Reflect on the wonderful times I've spent with my husband.

Create a place where I could safely preserve our date-night memorabilia.

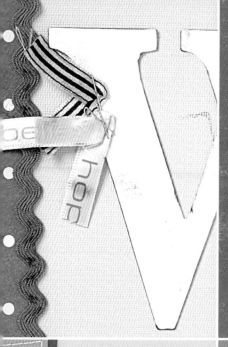

2003

As you finish each album, take a moment to add one final page, signed and dated by you. If desired, add notes about the messages in the album or a layout summary.

Express your creativity by looking for ways to tell your family memories outside of the traditional scrapbook page.

6

appreciate

*Show your appreciation
for the people in your life
with tribute albums.*

Birthday Tribute Album

When my mom's 75th birthday came around, my family decided to work together to create a wonderful gift for her: a series of three albums that celebrate our appreciation for the roles she's played in our lives, as a wife, a mother and a friend.

Supplies *Album, foam stamps, ribbon, ribbon charm and twill:* Making Memories; *Patterned papers and page accents:* Déjà Views, The C-Thru Ruler Company; *Labels:* DYMO; *Acrylic paint:* Delta Technical Coatings; *Computer font:* Source unknown; *Pen:* Zig Millennium, EK Success; *Other:* Brads, stitching and pop dots.

{ 1: PHOTOGRAPH }

I loved discovering priceless photographs of my parents that documented the early moments of their relationship together.

1.   My best friend!

2.   A great wife!!

3.   A wonderful mother!!!

4.   Remembers holidays and birthdays

5.   Complimentary to others

6.   Always the first to say hello

7.   Makes good chili

8.   Plants flowers every spring

9.   A good loser

10.   Lives beneath her means

{ 2: JOURNAL }

My dad wrote the journaling in this album, which includes 53 things he loves about my mom, one for every year that they've been married.

{ 3: PREPARE }

*I wanted it to be easy for my siblings to contribute to this
album, I created each layout as a simple spread.*

The Hanni Family

1. She is beautiful inside and out (Debbie)
2. Honest (Debbie)
3. Playful (Debbie)
4. Very thoughtful (Debbie)
5. Has tons of energy and likes to try new things (Mike)
6. A great initiator and peacemaker (Mike)
7. Great partner and caretaker to Dad (Mike)
8. Original (Chris)
9. Very positive: a good cook, story teller, and teacher (Chris)
10. Helpful and sensitive towards others (Chris)
11. I love the scent of her skin (Heather)
12. Helps me with crafts (Heather)
13. I love spending the night–it feels good and is a comfortable environment (Heather)
14. Bouncy, bright, funny and smiley (Jared)
15. A good planner (Jared)

{ 4: ORGANIZE }

*I sent blank layouts to my brothers and sisters and had
them add journaling and a photograph to their page.*

{ 5: REMEMBER }

A tribute album is a wonderful gift that will become a cherished heirloom.

{ 6: DESIGN }

Each layout in this book includes a handwritten note from one of Mom's friends.

Be Inspired

My Hero *by* Dee Gallimore-Perry

Supplies *Patterned papers:* Chatterbox (green and gray), Center City Designs (flowers and striped); *Vellum:* Chatterbox; *Rub-ons:* Making Memories and Creative Imaginations; *Tags, safety pins and ribbon:* Making Memories; *Labels:* me & my BIG ideas; *Rubber stamps:* Leave Memories; *Stamping ink:* Ranger Industries; *Embroidery thread:* DMC; *Dimensional adhesive:* Gloo, KI Memories; *Buttons:* 7gypsies; *Computer font:* Typewriter, downloaded from the Internet; *Other:* Sandpaper.

Lisa's album inspired me to:

Put my thoughts and feelings about my father into words.

Preserve my special photographs in a heartfelt way.

Dan & Diana

An Anniversary Tribute

My husband's parents constantly inspire me with the loving and caring example they've set for their children and grandchildren. This album is a celebration of their 40th wedding anniversary.

Supplies *Album:* K&Company; *Patterned papers:* K&Company; *Photo corners:* Canson; *Rub-ons and flowers:* Making Memories; *Brads:* Lasting Impressions for Paper; *Computer fonts:* CK Elegant, "Fresh Fonts" CD, *Creating Keepsakes;* Times New Roman, Microsoft Word; *Other:* Thread.

Start with a title page and a signed dedication page.

Make a list of pages you want to include in your tribute album.

Choose classic papers in subdued colors to create an elegant album.

Add photographs to the album that showcase the couple at different points in their marriage.

Ask the couple's children and grandchildren to handwrite notes of thanks to the couple.

An anniversary album can be a big project—it's okay to ask family members to help you!

Be Inspired

An Example to Live By *by* Mellette Berezoski

Supplies *Patterned papers:* Making Memories, Autumn Leaves and Creative Imaginations; *Flower, corner molding and brad:* Making Memories; *Index tab and rub-ons:* Autumn Leaves; *Bookplate and printed twill:* 7gypsies; *Circle accent:* K&Company; *Ribbon:* Making Memories and K&Company; *Buttons:* Junkitz; *Computer font:* Worn Machine, "Typewriter" CD, Autumn Leaves.

Becky's album inspired me to:

● Express my feelings of respect for my parents' courage and strength.

● Create a page with beautiful colors that keeps the focus on the photo of my parents.

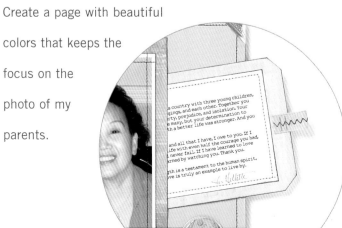

10 Ways to Scrapbook with Your Family

WE'VE BOTH TALKED with scrapbookers who have told us they feel overwhelmed by trying to stay caught up with their albums, pressured to create beautifully perfect pages.

But the fact is, you don't have to scrapbook alone. You're creating family scrapbooks— why not have your family pitch in and help you out? Here are 10 ways you can engage your family in the art of saving your family memories:

- Ask family members to write journaling on pages about what they've learned (for examples, see Lisa's "Live, Learn and Pass It On" album on page 76 or Becky's "School Years" album on page 107).

- Collect handwritten messages for tribute albums.

- Do you have an aunt, a sister, a sister-in-law or a nephew who scrapbooks? Consider getting together (in person or even online) to share pictures and to exchange scrapbook pages. It's always nice to have another perspective in your scrapbook!

- Create a free family blog (an online journal where you can post your thoughts and photographs) and invite family members to post thoughts, memories, highlights, life events, photographs, recipes and more on a regular basis. Print favorite blog entries and incorporate them into your scrapbook.

- While on vacation, have each family member write notes on postcards. Mail the postcards back home and use them as journaling on your vacation scrapbook pages.

- Give your children duplicate copies of your photographs and ask them to scrapbook the photographs in their own way.

- Ask your children to draw artwork to illustrate the pages you're scrapbooking.

- Realize that there is an inherent charm in "imperfect pages" (your child may not spell every word correctly, or your husband may have messy handwriting!).

- Create an album where you collect a variety of pages made by family members (this will show them that you do value their work and their help!).

- Combine your unused supplies into a family scrapbooking tote. Keep the tote in a place where it can be easily accessed at any time (you never know when your child may want to create a page instead of playing a video game or watching a movie!).

He Said, She Said

by Lisa Bearnson

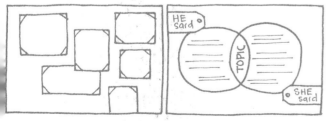

He Said, She Said Album

This album shows how much I appreciate my husband for both our similarities and our differences. This is really a humorous play on the "he said, she said" type of journaling.

Supplies *Album:* SEI

Cover
Supplies *Patterned papers:* Chatterbox and DieCuts with a View; *Letter stamps:* Rummage, Making Memories; *Rubber stamps:* Express Stamps, 7gypsies; *Stamping ink:* StazOn, Tsukineko; Distressing Ink, Ranger Industries; *Twill:* May Arts; *Computer fonts:* CK Surfer, "The Heritage, Vintage & Retro Collection" CD, *Creating Keepsakes*; AvantGarde, downloaded from the Internet.

Inside front cover
Supplies *Patterned paper:* Chatterbox; *Chipboard shapes:* Bazzill Chips, Bazzill Basics Paper; *Letter stamps:* Postmodern Design and PSX Design; *Stamping ink:* Distressing Ink, Ranger Industries; *Embroidery floss:* DMC.

Choose a list of topics to journal in the "he said, she said" format.

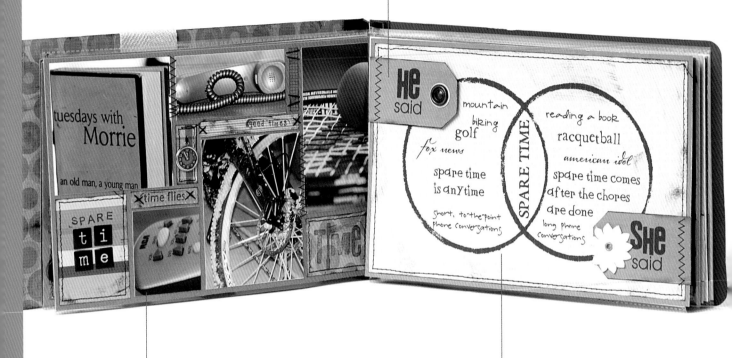

3: DESIGN

Design each page in a similar format, but alter the stitched lines on the layout to give each page a unique look.

2: ORGANIZE

Draw overlapping circles to fill with your journaling.

Start or end the album with a sweet photograph of the couple holding hands.

Take a second look at the tags on each page. I added a creative touch to each page by choosing different embellishments.

Consider stamping your answers or spelling them out with stickers or rub-on letters.

Be Inspired

Knowing Me, Knowing You *by* Karen Clauson

Supplies *Textured cardstock:* Bazzill Basics Paper; *Patterned paper and labeled words:* K&Company; *Flowers, metal photo corners and brads:* Making Memories; *Stamping ink:* ColorBox, Clearsnap; *Lettering template:* Paige Lowercase, QuicKutz.

Lisa's album inspired me to:

Ask my husband to write his answers to a set of questions so that I could compare his answers to my own.

Create a page that will teach our children how their parents are alike and yet different—individuals, yet a couple.

forty

years

Harold *Dan*
Higgins

Diana Christine
Stewart Higgins

Create an album that
celebrates cherished friendships
you've had over the years.
Add photographs,
names, dates and journaling
that shares what you value
about each friend.

VE YOU   I LOV

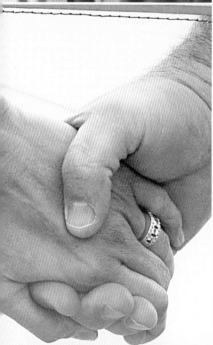

Allow your albums
to be a gathering place
where your friends and
family members can meet
and share stories.